Management self-development

A guide for managers, organisations and institutions

Tom Boydell

Prepared with the financial support of
the UNDP Inter-regional Programme

Management Development Series No. 21

International Labour Office   Geneva

ISBN 92-2-103958-7

First published 1985
Third impression 1986

ILO publications can be obtained through major booksellers or ILO local offices in many countries, or direct from ILO Publications, International Labour Office, CH-1211 Geneva 22, Switzerland. A catalogue or list of new publications will be sent free of charge from the above address.

CONTENTS

APPENDICES

INTRODUCTION

Why has this book been written? Or, from the point of view of the reader, what should you expect from reading it?

At any point in time, millions of managers all over the world are participating in some sort of training and development programme. To increase the impact of these programmes, both organisations employing managers and institutions where managers attend courses and seminars look for more effective training methodology. Great efforts are made to do more, and better, than merely to lecture on how to manage. The case method has brought life experience into the classroom. The computer has provided immediate feedback to decisions made in playing business games. Various organisation development methods have demonstrated that it is better to deal with whole teams than with isolated individuals, and that people learn best if involved in solving problems significant to their organisation.

Yet many of the current management development approaches and events fall short of expectations due to one common defect. They regard and treat managers as an object rather than a subject of the development process. Ignoring both experience and theories of adult learning, many organisations expose managers to a range of developmental activities, but fail to create conditions in which managers are keen to develop themselves. A training director's responsibility for developing managers is often substituted for every manager's responsibility for his own personal development. The results are disappointing in most cases. Managers may enjoy courses, but there is little transfer to work situations. A lot of talent and potential is never uncovered. The cost of training grows much more rapidly than the positive effects obtained.

But there are many other problems. Due to their growing cost, management courses are often accessible only to large and rich organisations. Managers living and working far from training institutions have very limited training opportunities. Some staff members may have to wait for many years before being offered a place in a course off-the-job, and so on.

This book has been written for three principal reasons. Firstly, to help increase managers' responsibility for their own development. Secondly, to directly assist those who are keen to develop themselves and therefore are looking for new techniques and resources for doing it. Thirdly, to provide some guidance to organisations and institutions keen to facilitate, encourage and assist managerial self-development.

Clientèle

Accordingly, the book is intended for the following types of reader.

Individual managers, and other persons interested in self-development, will find many guidelines, exercises and activities that they can actually use in their individual self-development. The exercises are designed so as to help you, the individual reader, to assess your own development needs, to negotiate your self-development with your organisation and then to develop various abilities, skills and attributes involved in being an effective manager. For example, some of the benefits drawn by experienced managers from various self-development exercises have included:

- learning new skills;

- improved job performance;

- making the best of themselves;

- career progression;

- self-satisfaction;

- greater recognition.

The book also includes a considerable number of practical guidelines for getting self-development established within an organisation. So, if you have a particular interest in, or responsibility for, improving management and developing managers in your organisation, you will find much that will help you in setting up a scheme that will be relevant not only to the needs of your managers, but that will also help to give your organisation the processes and relationships necessary for it to develop. These questions are very much in the province of what is called "organisational culture". It is well known that in some organisations people are keen to learn and develop themselves in any possible way. The climate and value system of other organisations inhibit any self-development effort and initiative. In which group is your organisation now and where do you want to be in the future?

Again, we can list a few examples of the effects of managerial self-development on organisations:

- increased efficiency;

- effective management succession plans;

- mobility of staff;

- ability to attract and retain high-calibre managers;

- ability to respond rapidly to changing circumstances and take new opportunities.

If you work in a management development institution (training centre, staff college, etc.) you will find a chapter on ways in which you can help your institution to take a role in initiating and promoting management self-development. On the surface, you may sense a conflict: is it not logical that if managers develop themselves through self-development programmes, this will reduce demand for training courses? Hence for your services? To avoid such a misunderstanding, our book explains how self-development can be integrated with various programmes run by management institutions, and used to enhance the effectiveness of management development at large.

Of course, the staff of management institutions should be familiar with the broad range of self-development methods described in this book, as well as with problems faced by organisations keen to support and help their staff in self-development. In addition, if you are a mangement teacher, trainer or consultant, you may be interested in trying out some new self-development method yourself!

As a result, an institution that decides to play an increased role in promoting self-development might expect to

- enhance its national or international reputation;

- be consulted and involved in important national and international programmes of human resource development;

- attract and retain high calibre staff;

- attract high quality and motivated participants;

- attract and obtain good levels of financial support for its activities;

- become a "centre of excellence", highly respected for its innovative approaches to learning and training.

How to use the book

Two important points concern all readers who will open this book.

Firstly, you can read about self-development and find its various methods and alternatives more or less interesting and useful. But if you are really keen to develop yourself, or to get a deep insight into a particular method to be able to recommend it to others and

Figure 1. Some possible responses to new ideas that clash with local culture

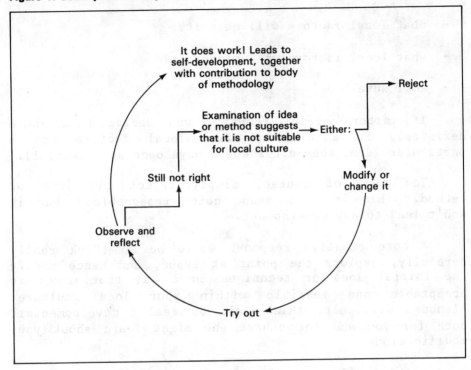

help them to use it, you must <u>experience self-development</u>. Hence if you are serious about it, try to do the exercises described in the book!

Secondly, you may find out that not only the organisational environment in which you work, but also your national culture has some implications for self-development. For example, the prevailing value system may or may not encourage individual initiative, dynamism, experimenting with new methods, and entrepreneurship in general. Or, a particular self-development method may be regarded as strange and hardly acceptable in a given cultural context.

You have to decide what is likely to work and therefore is worth trying. After all, it is your self-development. However, you should approach the book with an open mind - and an active one. When examining the various ideas and methods, try to be objective. Ask

5

- will this work here?

- what local factors will help it?

- what local factors will hinder it?

- am I sure?

If, after careful thought, you decide that there definitely is a clash between local factors and a particular item, then alternative ways open up (figure 1).

You can, of course, simply reject the idea or method. This is in a sense quite reasonable - but it won't lead to any development.

A more creative response would be to think really carefully, explore the point at issue, and hence modify the initial idea or technique in a way that makes it acceptable and feasible within your local culture. Although difficult, this would be really developmental, both for you and for others who might learn about your modifications.

A third alternative would be to take a risk and try out the new idea, more or less unchanged, even though you believe it might encounter local difficulty. Provided you do this very consciously - it is essential to think about all the issues beforehand - then the risk may be worth it. Surprising things may happen and you may learn and develop a lot.

We must stress that we are not suggesting a wild experiment with grossly unsuitable methods. Not at all - hence the need for careful consideration beforehand. It will also be a great help if you try very hard to be aware of what is happening when you try things out. To that end, some of this book's methods that describe ways of observing, reflecting and analysing your experiences will be particularly helpful.

These last two approaches will, we hope, lead to very real developments. By gradually trying out new ideas, modifying them for local conditions, trying them again, and so on, you will undoubtedly reinforce your own development. You will also be engaging in a process that will help your colleagues, by developing a system of management self-development principles and practices that are suited for your country – and which eventually become part of your culture.

This last point is quite important. One's local culture is in a constant process of slow but definite evolution. This process can be aided by careful, conscious attempts to experiment with new ideas; rejecting some, modifying and changing some, incorporating some. A difficult but worthwhile task.

Acknowledgements

The book was prepared in the framework of an international project entitled "Co-operation among management development institutions", implemented by ILO with the support of the United Nations Development Programme. One of the main objectives of the project is making useful experience, and information in innovative approaches to developing managers, available to the wide public of management institutions.

The author of the book, Tom Boydell, has been one of the pioneers of self-development, not only in the United Kingdom, his home country, but also in the developing countries. Many people have helped him in preparing this book, in a number of ways. Of particular help, however, has been Malcolm Leary, who has acted as a private coach to the author for some sections of the book, and Tom Boydell's spouse Gloria, the source of many of the insights and ideas in the book.

ILO Management Development Branch,
Geneva, August 1984.

SELF-DEVELOPMENT: WHAT AND WHY

1

1.1 Why should you read this book?

Perhaps you have seen advertisements for books, courses or seemingly magical products that more or less guarantee to bring you success, fame, fortune.

Well, we are not going to make such a claim here. No book can promise to bring about effortless self-development. What we can do, however, is to say that the methods and approaches described here are being used by an increasing number of managers throughout the world. This is because they have been shown to be relevant to the skills, qualities and attributes that are recognised as being characteristic of effective managers.

Perhaps you ought to ask yourself "why am I interested in self-development?" Your answers might include

- to get promotion;

- to do my current job more effectively;

- to get more satisfaction out of work (or out of my life).

Again, it would be dishonest to guarantee you any of these. However, there is no doubt that the qualities that can be developed by using this book will help you to achieve such goals. We say "can be developed", because again the outcomes are not automatic.

```
┌─────────────────────────────────────────────────────────────┐
│                                                               │
│      SELF-DEVELOPMENT IS HARD WORK AND BY DEFINITION          │
│                                                               │
│              IT IS YOUR RESPONSIBILITY!                       │
│                                                               │
└─────────────────────────────────────────────────────────────┘
```

We will look at these points later in more detail.
Before doing so perhaps it should also be noted that you
might find some of the approaches and methods a bit
strange. However, self-development requires, above all,
an open mind. These methods, including the "strange"
ones, are working for many managers in many countries.
So, if you want to try to be more systematic about your
development, take heart, read the book and above all have
a go at the activities!

1.2 What is self-development?

It is difficult to give a short, succinct definition
of self-development. Perhaps a more useful approach will
be to examine some of its characteristics.

One of these is that it involves the individual in
thinking for him or herself. We can apply this principle
here, by asking you, the reader, to think for yourself, to
use your own experience to work out your own ideas.

To help you, we will provide a structure for this
process. This reflects another principle of self-
development namely that working things out for yourself
can often be made easier by the intervention of someone
else, in the form of questions, structures for thinking
and feedback. Thus, you often need other people to help
with your self-development.

First, then, take a piece of paper and write down six
or seven key developmental events in your life. That is,
things that happened, experiences that in your opinion led
you to develop in some way. These events - which can be
from your worklife, your private life, or a mixture - may
have been very short or, in some cases, may have lasted
quite a time, such as several months. As long as you can
recognise them as definite, separate happenings, then that
is fine.

Figure 2. Characteristics of some key development events

(1) Events	(2) Outcomes	(3) Processes	(4) Feelings
1. 2. 3. etc.			

When you have identified six or seven of these, draw up a table such as that shown in figure 2.

In the first column, write down the developmental events that you have already identified. Then, in the second column, against each event, list the effects, the outcomes, the ways in which you think you developed as a result.

It is a bit difficult to explain what should be written in the third column. Broadly speaking, it refers to the activities or processes that you were involved in. These might be inner processes (such as thinking, sorting out confused ideas), outer ones (for example, talking with someone else) or a combination of both. For each event, there will almost certainly be several processes.

The fourth column is, perhaps, more straight-forward. For each event write down how you were feeling, what emotions you experienced, at the time. Again, you will probably find that there are several different feelings for each event.

Having completed the table, what can we make of it?

The outcomes of self-development; development of the self

First, look at what you wrote in the "outcomes" column. Clearly, it is impossible to predict here what

11

you will have written. However, it is possible to list some of the outcomes of other people's experiences, that have been collected from a number of self-development workshops. Examples include:

- acquiring a new skill;

- more confident;

- understanding of others;

- understanding how others see me;

- independence;

- starting to form my own values, thinking for myself;

- concern for other people (e.g. wife or husband, children).

Some of your entries in column 2 may well look a bit like some of these examples. In general, though, it is probable that, like the examples, your outcomes represent qualitative changes; new skills, different ways of seeing things, new understandings. It is less likely that they will refer to increases in something you already had, such as more knowledge on a familiar topic, or an improvement in a skill that you already possessed. Even if you have used words like "more confidence", this is really a qualitative change; it feels different, rather than just a topping up in confidence level.

Self-development, then, involves personal change; new abilities, different outlooks, new feelings. Although as a result you feel you are a better person, or a better manager, this is due to these new qualities, rather than to mere improvement and refinement of skills and abilities that you already had, adding more of the same. These outcomes, then, of personal change, might be said to be development of the self.

Development in terms of thinking, feeling and willing

At this stage, before looking at the processes of self-development (i.e. development by self), it will be useful to consider a particular way of classifying these

12

qualitative changes, involving three basic inner activities - thinking, feeling and willing (these processes will be referred to again many times in later chapters).

The terms virtually speak for themselves. Thinking concerns our ideas, beliefs, concepts, theories. Feeling also includes our emotions and moods. And willing is concerned with action - what we really are prepared to do (or are not prepared to do, as the case may be).

We will return to these inner activities later, in chapter 2. In the meantime, though, they can be used as part of a framework when looking at the qualitative changes of development. This is summarised in table 1, but a few explanatory words might be helpful (a questionnaire based on table 1 and designed as an aid to self-assessment is reproduced in appendix 3).

Four main areas or aspects of development have been taken - health, skills, action and sense of identity.

Let us start with health - a sound mind in a sound body. In this context, you possess a healthy or sound mind if you are neither dogmatic, too full of your own views, nor over-reliant on other people's ideas - although you are prepared to listen to others, to respect their view, even if you do not agree with them. Thus, healthy thinking is characterised by possessing a system of coherent and consistent ideas and beliefs which, whilst viewed with an open mind are not likely to be changed from moment to moment.

A healthy mind can cope with both detail and with generality. That is, you can look at details, notice them, without becoming bogged down, and you can also grasp general principles, get an overview of the situation, without ignoring or overlooking the more detailed aspects.

The effect of your ideas and actions on other people is also considered, thus leading to a set of personal standards and moral values. Here too, therefore, we find philosophical, religious and spiritual beliefs.

What of a "healthy" feelings life? Certainly one characteristic is an awareness of your feelings, and of the effect they are having on you. In contrast, it is

13

Table 1. Qualitative outcomes of development

FOCUS OF DEVELOPMENT; aspects of the self	OUTCOMES OF SELF-DEVELOPMENT		
	Thinking	Feeling	Willing
HEALTH; sound mind in a sound body	Undogmatic and open-minded commitment to coherent and consistent ideas and beliefs; at the same time an ability to live with ambiguities and paradoxes. Ability to handle both detail and overviews. Personal standards. Values. Morality. Philosophical, religious and spiritual beliefs.	Awareness and acknowledgement of feelings. Balance — inner and outer. Integration. Inner calm.	Nutrition. Diet. Physical fitness. Healthy habits and life-style.
SKILLS	Mental and conceptual skills e.g. job knowledge, memory, logic, creativity, intuition.	Social skills. Artistic skills. Expressive skills.	Technical skills. Job skills. Physical skills. Mechanical skills.
ACTION IN THE WORLD — GETTING THINGS DONE; motivation and courage	Ability to make choices and sacrifices; to say no.	Ability to manage, make sense of, and transform set-backs, frustration, disappointment, unhappiness and suffering.	Ability to go out, to take initiatives, to step in.
IDENTITY; "It's all right, it's good, to be me"	Knowledge, awareness and understanding of self.	Acceptance of self, in spite of weaknesses. Rejoicing in strengths.	Self motivation, inner compass, purpose in life.

unhealthy to suppress feelings, or to deny having them, since this usually leads to problems - a suppressed feeling nearly always comes out eventually, in a number of unwelcome ways, such as uncontrollable responses (losing one's temper, for example), deteriorating relationships with others, tension, nervous complaints, sleepless nights, or a host of illnesses. This is not to say that it is healthy to let your feelings take charge of you; far from it. After all, do you have feelings or do feelings have you? No, a balance is required, such that you are aware of your feelings, and acknowledge them, without allowing yourself to be overwhelmed by them.

Healthy feelings are also related to another aspect of balance - that is, balance between work and play, professional life and home life, thinking activities and doing activities, material or wordly interests and spiritual interests. In any of these cases an excess in one direction, at the expense of the other, can lead to tension, stress and their consequences. Development, therefore should include examining these aspects of one's life, looking for what is unbalanced, and taking steps to improve things.

Three other aspects of balance should also be mentioned. The first is an inner balance, or calmness, that can usually be brought about by various types of contemplation, meditation, and yoga.

The second is a balance between, or integration of, the thinking, feeling and willing processes themselves. For example, someone who is always thinking about things, but never doing anything about them, is out of balance. Conversely, the over-eager doer, who leaps into action without giving the matter any thought at all, is also out of balance. Again, someone who spends all their time expressing feelings, pouring out emotions to everybody, would be more in balance if he or she thought about the meaning of the feelings and what was causing them. So achieving these types of balance is another focus for development.

Finally, there needs to be a balance between the four developmental focuses. That is, between the time and effort you spend on developing your health, your skills, your actions, and your identity. Some people, for example, become "fitness freaks", spending so much time on physical exercise that they have no time for skills, or for doing anything useful in society, or for self-awareness. Others put all their effort into self-awareness techniques, at the expense of health, skills and action. Others again are so active getting things done that their health gives way. There therefore needs to be this "vertical" balance between outer and inner, between working on inner development, and on doing things at work, in the family and in the community.

What about "healthy willing"? Here we are dealing basically with physical health, which is affected by things such as diet, nutrition, healthy habits (e.g. regular sleep, relaxation activities, exercise, refraining from smoking) and fitness.

Turning now to skills, in the thinking area we need to develop a variety of mental and conceptual skills, including memorising, logic, job and technical knowledge, creativity and, more difficult perhaps, intuition.

The area of "doing" or "willing skills" is where we find physical, technical and job skills (for example, using equipment, manipulating materials, dexterity, and so on).

The middle column – "feeling skills" – is an interesting one. Here perhaps lies the difference between a skilled performer (willing skills) and a real artist – the latter is bringing his or her feelings into the situation. Thus, the really artistic painter, sculptor, musician, weaver, batikist, is translating feelings into action. This is where mere technique is not enough – the extra ingredient of personal feeling is vital. As far as managers are concerned, this is mainly true in the area of social skills – dealing with people. A purely mechanical, technique-oriented approach to handling people is just not sufficient, whether we deal with listening, communicating, understanding, helping, negotiating, motivating, disciplining, loving, or whatever. These activities are inextricably bound up with our feelings, both about ourselves and the other(s) involved, so that we must try to become social artists, rather than social mechanics. Hence the social skills entry in the feelings column.

16

The possession of skills is not, of course, in itself any guarantee that you will actually get things done. This requires a further, motivating element and brings us to the next row of entries in the table. First, to get things done, you very often have to make a choice between alternatives. Sometimes this is quite straightforward, as one alternative stands out as being clearly the most desirable one. Often, however, all the possible choices have some advantages and some disadvantages. Furthermore, some of the "good" features of a particular option may seem extremely attractive, compared with some less pleasant aspects of another possibility, even though overall the latter is probably a better choice. Getting things done, therefore, often involves giving up some desirable alternatives, saying no to those, or making sacrifices for the sake of a better overall choice.

When things are going well, and are enjoyable, action is quite easy. Unfortunately, however, things often go wrong, causing setbacks, frustration, or even unhappiness and suffering. In these circumstances it is all too easy to give up. A more developed person, however, is able to continue the struggle. He or she does not give up in the face of difficulty, but carries on, learning perhaps from the frustration and unhappiness, making sense of it. This is the application of courage and motivation in the feelings life.

Getting things done also requires you to be able to take initiatives, to be "proactive" - i.e. take steps for yourself rather than waiting for something to happen, or to be told what to do (to be "reactive").

In a sense, then, we have seen that with a platform of health - physical and mental - we can develop skills; with motivation and courage, these skills can be translated into action. As a result, we develop a sense of identity - a feeling that "it is all right to be me", as someone on a recent development course put it. This acceptance of yourself is accompanied by knowledge and understanding of yourself, and also by an inner drive, inner direction, a sense that there is a purpose in life.

There is not, of course, a complacent acceptance, which would indeed be anti-developmental. No - it involves recognition of weaknesses, without hating yourself, or becoming despondent, because of them; at the same time you resolve either to improve on them, or to make the best of an imperfect situation. You also recognise, acknowledge and rejoice in your strengths, without becoming over-confident or boastful, or on the other hand, self-deprecating and full of false modesty.

Perhaps, then, this is a summary of what self-development is about: building up health, skills, motivation, courage, and sense of identity and purpose in life.

Personal growth or management development?

So far there has been little reference to the manager as such. Rather, the outcomes summarised in table 1 could really be said to lead to development as a person, rather than as a manager.

Clearly, though, managers are people! And there is today an increasing recognition of the link between personal and professional growth. In the field of management, this is reflected in new ways of considering managerial competence and effectiveness.

One such way involves three main levels of competence, as follows.

At the first level, the manager is behaving like a technician. He or she is able to carry out standard routines and prescribed procedures, and can use techniques that they have been taught, can remember facts, can understand other peoples' explanations of ideas and theories. There is an ability to respond to things "correctly" - that is, in the ways that have been laid down, taught, explained, or through the use of habits and knacks that have been acquired, usually through unthinking trial and error.

Now there is nothing wrong in being able to perform in this way. Many jobs call for much of that sort of ability (a lot of what is called "administration" is like this). However, it often is not sufficient, because being a manager requires something extra.

18

This extra can be seen at the next stage of development, when the manager is behaving like a professional. At this stage, new factors start to come into play. There is an increasing element of "making abilities my own" - of developing my own style of doing things. Knowledge becomes more personal, and systems of knowledge are built up, rather than mere collections of unrelated facts. Often these systems require an ability to handle ideas that are, apparently, contradictory - to begin to synthesise, to think in terms of "both ... and ...", rather than "either ... or ...". Conscious choices are made from alternative courses of action in an ambiguous situation. These situations, unlike those at the "technician" level, are such that there is no standard, correct predetermined solution. Instead, the manager has to monitor his or her own decisions, at the same time developing an increasing level of self-awareness, of conscious learning from experience. There is thus an emphasis on making personal sense, out of what is happening. More creative ideas can be generated; whole new ways of looking at things are tried out - new ways of tackling old problems, as well as new problems.

It is at this stage, then, that we can see the sort of developmental outcomes from table 1 coming into play. We can take this process to a further stage, at which we might say that the manager is behaving like a really mature person, which is similar to the "professional" stage, with an important extra feature. This addition is that there is now a real personal understanding of what it means for me to be a manager, involving an exploration of the balance between me-as-manager, me-as-husband or wife, me-as-parent, me-as-member of the community, and so on. It is at this stage, too, that questions of personal standards, values and morals come fully into play. Often the manager has to resolve difficult conflicts between his or her values and those prevailing in the organisation. For example, you might find that you are being asked to treat your subordinates in a way that you consider to be morally wrong. Or you may be ordered to tell lies about what is going on in your organisation, in order to defend it against criticism from outside - criticism that might well be justified, in your opinion.

Sometimes, too, one has to face up to the realities of "professional deformation", whereby certain aspects of people's work either force them into behaving in ways that are basically against their fundamental personal make up, or cause them to become unbalanced in one of the senses described earlier. For example, your job may require you to think so much that you have little time left for actually doing anything; or you may become so highly skilled in a physical sense that you spend all your time on physical, technical tasks, cutting yourself off from other people and consequently not developing your social skills. The "mature-person" manager becomes aware of this, and takes steps to redress the balance.

The phrase "mature-person" manager is a bit of a mouthful. Since this third level involves so much of the self in being a manager, we might say that it involves expressing yourself fully in a managerial role. You will recall that earlier this element of personal expression was identified as a characteristic of artistic skills, so perhaps a better phrase for this level might be "manager as artist". This takes the managing away from being a systematic, mechanical process ("techniques and science of management") into a whole new level of the "art of management", as below:

manager as technician   :   techniques of management

manager as professional :   science of management

manager as artist   :   art of management.

As should be clear, moving through these three levels (techniques – science – art) increasingly involves the self, the whole person, in being a manager. They represent the application of the outcomes of development of self.

In the complex, rapidly changing world of today, it is no longer good enough to be a manager-as-technician (level 1). There is a most urgent need for managers-as-professionals (level 2), and managers-as-artists (level 3). Only with the flexible, creative, responsible characteristics of these two levels will we be able to manage the complicated world we find ourselves in.

This is, of course, in no way intended to decry the first level. All managers need to be able to work in these ways from time to time. However, this is no longer sufficient - developing into the second and third levels increases your repertoire of abilities, thereby preparing you to work in a wider range of complex situations.

We can see here, too, another example of the balance that is a key part of healthy development. As already mentioned, one aspect of this is the balance between inner and outer life - working on your personal self, and working on tasks in the world. Ideally, therefore, the development of inner, personal qualities should be seen as a preparation for tasks that need to be done - in your organisation, or your family, or your community. The really effective manager is aware of his or her responsibility for such tasks, and is therefore prepared to develop the inner qualities that are required.

1.3 Self-development processes

Development by self

It will be useful now to return to your personal version of figure 2, in which you wrote down the characteristics of some of your key developmental events.

So far we have concentrated on the outcomes of these events (column 2), thence looking at ideas about development of self. Now we can look at the processes involved, by considering what you wrote in column 3 of the table.

As with the outcomes column, the entries in this one will, of course, vary from person to person. Some examples from other managers include:

- solving a problem;

- working out the answer for myself;

- trying out a new way of doing something;

- thinking about something that has happened;

- giving up old ideas;

- taking a risk;

- working through a deep emotion, such as disappointment, grief;

- facing up to a new challenge;

- reading;

- obtaining information and using it;

- applying a new idea.

One thing that these have in common - as, probably, will your entries - is that they are basically active. True, the activity may be as much mental as physical, but none the less the person is personally involved. He or she is not passively being told things, given instructions.

There are, of course, exceptions to this. None the less, it is likely that the majority of your processes involved you in doing something, mentally or physically. And very often you will find that in cases where you were relatively passive (for example, when someone explained something to you) you then had to apply this information to a real task or problem. This is another characteristic of development - it is nearly always related to something that happens in your real life or it involves an important, significant issue, problem, or task with which you are confronted. It rarely takes place as the result of going on a conventional course, covering someone else's syllabus in order to pass an exam or acquire a qualification.

This last point is very important, and needs emphasising. Self-development rarely (but sometimes) occurs as the result of learning abstract, academic, theoretical ideas from a syllabus laid down by somebody else. Furthermore, on the relatively few occasions when it does come about in this way, this is due more to the process (for example, learning to think) than to the content.

This is not to say that theory as such is un-important or irrelevant. Far from it. The important

Figure 3. The development cycle

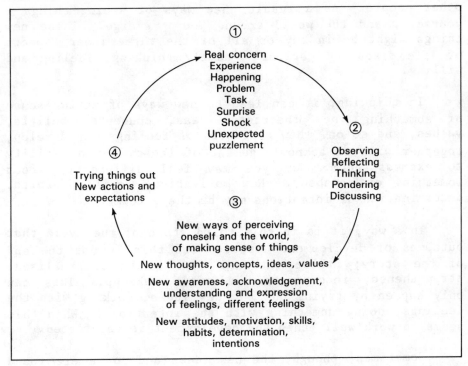

① Real concern
Experience
Happening
Problem
Task
Surprise
Shock
Unexpected
puzzlement

② Observing
Reflecting
Thinking
Pondering
Discussing

④ Trying things out
New actions and
expectations

③ New ways of perceiving
oneself and the world,
of making sense of things

New thoughts, concepts, ideas, values

New awareness, acknowledgement,
understanding and expression
of feelings, different feelings

New attitudes, motivation, skills,
habits, determination,
intentions

thing, however, is to make any theory personal, by working with it in a way that is important to you. To become alive, theory must be integrated with personal experience.

Self-development normally comes about through the person making sense of some actual experience, and/or tackling a significant problem that matters to him or her, that is, it affects his or her work or life.

The way this happens can be shown diagrammatically, as in figure 3. The developmental cycle starts with a real concern. This may be a problem or task; it may be surprise or puzzlement, or even shock, when something has happened that was unexpected does not seem to make sense.

The next stage in the cycle involves thinking about the problem or experience, working with possible

23

explanations and ideas, perhaps discussing these with other people. As a result, new ways of seeing things - yourself, and the world around you - emerge. These new things might be in any or all of the three inner aspects of life discussed earlier - namely thinking, feeling and willing.

In thinking, it can lead to new ways of making sense of something, new theories, ideas, concepts, beliefs, values, and so on. New awareness of feelings may develop, together with an acknowledgement of these, and an ability to express them. Or you may feel differently about something or somebody. New motivations, skills, habits, determination or intentions may be the outcome.

In a way, it is in this third stage of the cycle that outcomes of development appear. But this is not the end of the story; these outcomes need to be internalised, strengthened, incorporated in one's make-up. This can only happen by trying out the new ideas, working with the feelings, doing something with the intentions. When this seems to work well, then the development is reinforced.

Sometimes, though, the new ideas and so on are found not to work after all. Or they are only partially valid. In these cases, a further puzzlement, surprise or problem arises, and hence the cycle starts over again.

As described, the developmental cycle is shown as starting with the problem or experience. However, sometimes it starts at stage 3 - new ideas, skills and so on are fed in, by reading, or by instruction. However, they very often stay there, as it were trapped at the bottom of the cycle. It is only when they are applied to a real issue that their personal meaning becomes apparent. In any case, it is very likely that an idea presented in this way will not be quite right for your particular situation. You have to work with it, try it out, practise (stage 3) until something happens (stage 1) that you have to think about for yourself (stage 2). And so on.

So, even in cases where new ways of seeing, feeling or doing are presented (as by an instructor, or in a

24

book), development will only take place if you respond actively, working with these new ways, sorting out for yourself what they mean for you.

There is, too, a link between this way of looking at development and the levels of management that have been described earlier. The manager as a technician is more or less the one who is stuck at the bottom of the cycle. These managers are good enough at receiving ideas from others, but they are not able to go round the rest of the cycle. It is this ability to work things out for oneself, to learn from experience, to tackle new problems, that forms the essence of the difference between managing by techniques and the others (science of management and art of management). It is, as it were, the "extra ingredient".

Broad strategies for self-development

We have seen, then, that the outcomes of self-development represent development of the self, and that to achieve this it is necessary to adopt processes that involve development by the self.

Ways of doing this - i.e. guidance on development by the self - will be described in chapters 3 to 8. However, at this point it might be useful to highlight two main approaches or strategies that can be used. These are:

- seeking out a range of experiences, problems and issues, to use as vehicles for development; that is, increase the amount of activity in stage 1 of the development cycle;

- improving your ability to develop from experiences; that is, acquire the skills and outlooks required in stages 2, 3 and 4 of the development cycle.

Of course, we encounter many experiences and problems anyway, without going out looking for them. Often, though, these really represent repetitions of similar experiences - hence the old saying that for many people "ten years' experience is really one years' experience, repeated ten times". So it is not only the "quantity" of experience, but also the nature, or quality, that is important. Chapters 3 to 8 give descriptions of a number of ways of improving and increasing the quality of your experience in order to provide good opportunities for development. The same chapters also look at ways of improving your ability to develop from your experiences – those that occur naturally, as everyday work and living, and those that you set out to make happen.

The role of other people in your self-development

It will now be useful to highlight another aspect of self-development processes. Looking again at your original table (from figure 2), how many of the events involved other people? It is very likely that many of them did so. For one of the interesting things about this is that very often you need other people to help with your self-development.

Other people may be involved in the experience, or be part of the problem, issue, surprise. They can help by giving you feedback, by questioning, sharing, discussing, helping you to reflect and think. They may support you when the process is difficult or uncomfortable; or they may challenge you, confront you, forcing you to reconsider your ideas.

Who are these other people? Usually they can be friends, family, colleagues, fellow learners. Often these last are particularly appropriate, as you can help them whilst they help you. It can be a very good idea to form a small group – a self-help group – of friends or colleagues who want to help each other to develop. Alternatively, you can make an arrangement with one particular person to meet regularly and share experiences. Such a person might be described as your "speaking partner". We will say more about both self-help groups and speaking partners in chapter 8.

Usually, it is not necessary for the other person or people to be professional trainers or management development specialists. Nearly all the methods of self-development described in chapters 3 to 8 can be done either entirely on your own, or with a speaking partner(s) who is an "ordinary" person, a friend, a colleague. The methods do not require trainers to run them for you. (There are a couple of exceptions, as will be seen later.) Of course, if you do have access to a skilled trainer, then there is no harm in discussing things with him or her. But anyway, no trainer can possibly find time to talk in detail with every manager.

So this is another aspect of development by self. Not only are you active in the process, generating your own meanings, understandings and so on (as in figure 2), but you are not dependent on the availability or skills of training specialists. Certainly it can be helpful, but it is not essential, to share your development with someone else, but this person or persons can be anyone of your choice, whom you want to work with in this way. Really, you can be independent of professional training staff - although they can be very helpful.

Is self-development selfish?

Other people, then, can help you with your development. Equally, of course, you can help them with theirs, by listening, giving feedback, sharing experiences and so on.

There is also another important aspect of the link between your development and that of other people. If you are going to make changes, how will other people react? Will they be pleased, or do they like you as you are? Or if you decide that to develop you will have to change your job, or go away for a year on an overseas course, how will this affect other people, such as your family?

There is a real dilemma here. On the one hand, self-development involves you in deciding what to do, and how to do it, in being independently in control of your own life.

On the other hand, a developed person is not selfish, but considers the feelings and wishes of others.

Perhaps this is one of the hardest of paradoxes to resolve. Be my own captain? Or consider others? Perhaps an important step in managing this problem is to become aware of it. When faced with a problem, try to identify who is trying to influence you (see appendix 1). At the same time, who else will be affected by your decision - what will they be thinking, feeling and willing if you choose to act in a certain way?

Then try to balance these two forces when coming to your decision.

Sometimes, perhaps, you might decide that consideration for others means that you ought not to take some particular action - for example, not go on that course overseas. But in the end, you have to decide - and you have to realise that you have decided. It is no use then being resentful, blaming others for getting in your way, and so on. Make the decision consciously, having considered all the factors (and, probably, listened to your inner self, as explained in chapter 4), and then stick with the decision.

Self-assessment

Another aspect of development by self is that you assess yourself. Although this process may be helped by discussions with others, it is up to you to decide what you want to try to achieve. You are not being ordered to do it, by your boss or by anyone else. Chapter 2 provides a number of alternative methods of self-assessment.

Self-development - often a difficult process

Now for a last look at what you wrote in the figure 2 table. This time it is the last column that we are interested in - your feelings. It is very likely that these will be a mixture of nice and nasty feelings, with, more likely than not, more nasty ones than nice.

Why is this? Looking back at figure 3 - the development cycle - will help to explain. Stage 1 of the cycle involves surprises, shocks, puzzles, problems and so on, and these are very likely to be accompanied by a variety of "unpleasant" feelings, including confusion, worry, fear, anxiety, shock, although sometimes you may be excited, or curious. These feelings may continue into stage 2, although often, at the time of sudden understanding, you may well feel exhilarated, relieved, comforted, reassured.

So a mixture of feelings is to be expected. But it is perhaps more important to realise that negative feelings are not unusual; indeed, they are more to be expected. Development is at times a painful process.

Hopefully, though, if you are aware of this fact - that development is often painful - it will help you to

Figure 4. Personal qualities required for self-development

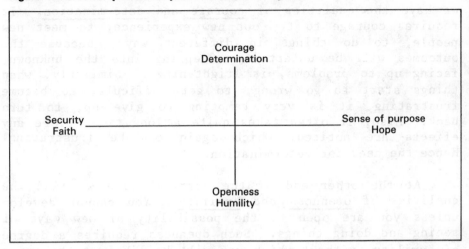

continue, not to give up. In a sense development requires faith – faith that the difficult aspects will be overcome and will lead to really significant learning. And, as has already been mentioned, discussing and sharing things with somebody else will often make the experience easier and more fruitful.

Perhaps this all sounds a bit grim, a bit fore-boding! That is certainly not the intention. Self-development is in many ways most exciting, satisfying and fulfilling. However, it is important to stress that it very often involves difficult patches, requiring hard work, determination and commitment. There is no easy route, or short cut. No one else can do the hard work for you – after all, we are talking about <u>self</u>-development, not job instruction. But there certainly are ways to make it somewhat easier and more effective, and various approaches are described in chapters 3 to 8.

Some personal qualities required for self-development

Self-development, then, involves hard work! Four main personal qualities seem to be needed to provide the drive for such work. These qualities are illustrated in figure 4.

As drawn in the figure, these qualities can be seen as being on two dimensions.

Let us first look at the vertical pair. At one end we have the qualities of courage and determination. It requires courage to try out new experience, to meet new people, to do things in different ways, because the outcomes will be uncertain. Stepping into the unknown, facing up to problems, is frightening. Similarly, when things start to go wrong, to get difficult, to become frustrating, it is very tempting to give up, to turn back. Also, it often takes quite a long time before any effects are noticed, which again can be frustrating. Hence the need for determination.

At the other end of the vertical line we find the qualities of openness and humility. You cannot develop unless you are open to the possibility of new ways of seeing and doing things. Such openness requires a degree of humility, without which you will be likely to become a "know-all", who is, in fact, trapped by feelings of superiority.

Of course, it is possible to overdo the openness, to become too humble. This leads to feelings of inferiority and lack of confidence, with a belief that everybody else's ideas are better than your own. This will not be conducive to development.

Similarly, it is possible to be too courageous (becoming foolhardy and reckless), or too determined (leading to stubbornness). Again, these conditions are likely to get in the way of development.

Let us now look at the horizontal line in figure 4. In a way this can be considered to be a time dimension. At the left hand end we have your relationship with the past - has it left you with a sense of security, with some sort of inner faith that things will work out all right eventually? If so, you are more likely to be able to face up to developmental challenges, to keep going when nothing seems to be improving, than if, as a result of unhappy experiences, you are insecure, with a feeling that there really is not much hope.

In a similar way, the right-hand end of this dimension refers to the future. You need something in the form of an objective, or purpose, or at least a sense of wanting to move in a general direction, even if that direction appears to be pretty vague. Without at least an awareness of a sense of purpose, or some degree of hope that you will be able to develop, you will again be stuck, like those who see no point in changing and developing, because they are quite content to remain as they are.

We must be careful not to overdo these qualities as well. Excessive security and faith can turn into complacency and fatalism - a sense that "what will be will be", and therefore there is nothing to be done but to sit around and see what happens. In the same way, a distorted sense of purpose can lead to fanaticism and an exaggerated view of one's own importance.

So, to develop we need

- courage, determination but not recklessness, foolhardiness, stubbornness;

- openness, humility but not inferiority;

- security, faith, but not complacency, fatalism;

- purpose, hope, but not fanaticism, self-aggrandisement.

Paradoxically, we must note that these qualities are to some extent the outcomes of development. So to develop, you must have developed already!

In fact, of course we all have developed already. The point we are now making is that to develop further you need to make more conscious use of these qualities, and also to try to improve them. Appendix 4 includes an approach (biography work) that might be helpful here - particularly with the security/purpose factors. And in chapter 5 there is a description of methods for working on courage and openness. The more you use such methods, and develop in other ways, so will your courage, openness, security and sense of purpose improve; and so on - a positive circle!

Having said that, it must again be stressed that there is no neat, ready answer for self-development. It is hard work, and progress is often apparently

Figure 5. Skills involved in self-development

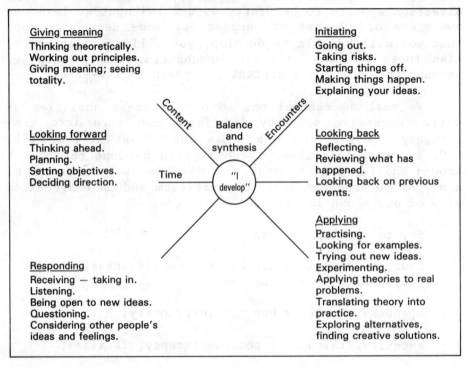

Giving meaning
Thinking theoretically.
Working out principles.
Giving meaning; seeing
totality.

Initiating
Going out.
Taking risks.
Starting things off.
Making things happen.
Explaining your ideas.

Looking forward
Thinking ahead.
Planning.
Setting objectives.
Deciding direction.

Balance
and
synthesis

Content

Encounters

Time

"I
develop"

Looking back
Reflecting.
Reviewing what has
happened.
Looking back on previous
events.

Applying
Practising.
Looking for examples.
Trying out new ideas.
Experimenting.
Applying theories to real
problems.
Translating theory into
practice.
Exploring alternatives,
finding creative solutions.

Responding
Receiving — taking in.
Listening.
Being open to new ideas.
Questioning.
Considering other people's
ideas and feelings.

negligible. Sometimes the changes, when they come, happen very quickly, with sudden flashes of meaning. At others, the change is so gradual that you do not notice it, until, perhaps, someone makes a comment to you.

There is also another important point to make here - the principle of readiness. For every one of us there are some developmental steps that we are not yet ready to take. Deciding not to work on these is therefore not running away from something, but is sensible prudence. It is not easy, unfortunately, to decide whether you really are not yet ready or whether you should in fact take the risk and jump in. Some of the methods described in chapter 4 (those in the section called "listening to your inner self") may be of help in this situation.

Some skills involved in self-development

So far we have examined the basic self-development

process (figure 3) and some personal qualities required (figure 4). We can now look at some of the skills involved. These are shown in figure 5.

As you can see, the skills are shown on three axes - encounters, content and time.

At one end of the "encounters" line we have outward experiences, usually with other people (occasionally with objects). These involve skills such as taking actions, doing things that are sometimes risky (because of the danger of failure, or because the outcomes are uncertain, ambiguous), starting things off and initiating, making things happen, explaining your ideas to other people. Conversely, at the other end we have inner directed experience, taking in ideas. Skills required for this include listening, maintaining an open mind, questioning, respecting views that differ from your own, and showing consideration for other people's feelings.

Now let us look at the "content" line. The top end is the area of theory, and you therefore require such related skills as the ability to think theoretically, working with abstract principles and ideas, conceptualising. In contrast, at the bottom end we have application and practicality - more "down to earth", as it were. This requires skills like trying out new ideas, experimenting, applying theories to real problems, looking for examples, finding creative solutions.

Thirdly, we have the "time" dimension. At the left, there is forward planning, thinking ahead, setting objectives, deciding your direction. And, at the other end, we have a backward past orientation, involving skills of reflecting, reviewing what has happened, looking back on previous events.

In order to develop, all these skills are required (a questionnaire to help you assess your level of each of these skills is given in appendix 1). Clearly, there are times when it will be more important to think ahead, say. At others, experimenting will be called for. And so on. So a key central ability is to decide which of the other skills are required at a particular time, and then to call these into play.

1.4 Why is self-development needed?

There are several reasons or situations that call for a self-development approach.

First, there is the effect of self-development. You will recall that in the section of this chapter headed "Personal growth or management development?", we showed how the outcomes of self-development were in fact those very qualities, skills and so on that are needed in the higher stages of managerial effectiveness. So methods of self-development, such as those described in this book, are those that are required for real competence and effectiveness as a manager. Furthermore, it is this type of effectiveness that is needed to manage the complicated, changing and challenging world we live in. We can no longer rely on standard answers, set procedures, laid down routines. Organisations today need to be more flexible, innovative, responsive and responsible to the community. It is only at the second and third levels of effectiveness that we find such qualities. In other words, the self-development approach is the one that we need if our organisations are to survive, let alone to flourish, in today's circumstances.

Not everybody will share this view. You will very probably encounter scepticism and opposition to new ideas, new ways of doing things. Such hostility can be very frustrating, and at times you will probably become discouraged. However, since one of the features of a developed person (table 1) is to be able to keep going in the face of set-backs, then these very difficulties can themselves become a source or vehicle for further development.

Now obviously this is easier said than done! These abilities are not easily come by. None the less, some of the methods described in chapters 3 to 8 can at least offer some help in this direction.

At the same time, are you perhaps the cause of someone else feeling frustrated? Are you behaving to others in ways that you find unhelpful when your boss does them to you? It is very easy to complain about the way people will not listen to you, will not allow you to try out new ideas, and so on. But do you listen to people, do

34

you allow them to try new ideas? Again, chapter 8 can give some guides on working on these aspects of your development.

We have also been discussing development by self, using processes and methods in which you are deciding how, when and where to develop, as well as being actively engaged in the actual developmental cycle. Being independent of trainers, course timetables and the like is another advantage of self-development. It is up to you when to learn; you can arrange to engage in developmental activities (such as reading, working on structured exercises, etc., as in chapter 3) at a time and place convenient to yourself. This can be at a set time each day (lunchtime, or in the evening), or when you find you have a spare hour or two. You can do it at home or at work.

Similarly, of course, this means that self-development approaches can be used by managers in isolated settings. The resources required are relatively simple, cheap, and easy to come by. Most of the methods in later chapters really only require yourself and some time, although often paper and pen or pencil are also useful. None of them involves "high technology" (such as videos, electronic gadgets, films, computers, projectors), and only a small percentage require groups of other people. It is certainly not necessary to wait to go on a course, either overseas or at an oversubscribed local institution. So, in the main, even if you are working in an isolated setting, you can still use the majority of the methods - although, as has already been stated, it often helps to have someone to talk to about your progress, to share ideas and feelings with. However, this is not absolutely essential.

These advantages - simple technology, independence of complex resources, flexibility in time and location - make this a particularly useful approach for use in developing countries.

Finally, there is another very important advantage. Since it involves you in looking at yourself, working on your issues and problems, thinking out your own solutions, developing your health, skills, application and sense of identity, the self-development approach is virtually guaranteed to be relevant to you. Unlike many other methods of training, there is much less likelihood of inappropriate ideas being introduced into your situation - ideas which are either irrelevant, useless, or positively harmful.

In summary, then, self-development requires hard work. It calls for qualities such as faith, hope, openness and courage, and involves the use of a number of skills, and often requires quite a time before showing results. In that sense it certainly does not offer a simple solution to all our problems. On the other hand it does possess certain very important advantages, namely in that it

- leads to the sort of higher levels of effectiveness that are particularly important for managers;

- focuses on relevant problems and outcomes, appropriate for situations in which you find yourself;

- relies mainly on simple and accessible resources.

1.5 Suggestions for further reading

Boydell, T.H.; Pedler, M.J. Self-development bibliography. Bradford, MCB, 1979.

Burgoyne, J.G.; Boydell, T.H.; Pedler, M.J. Self-development: Theory and applications for practitioners. London, Association of Teachers of Management, 1978.

Juch, B. Personal development. Chichester, Wiley, 1983.

Lievegoed, B. Phases. London, Rudolph Steiner Press, 1979.

Livingstone, J.S. "Myth of the well-educated manager", in Harvard Business Review, Jan.-Feb. 1971.

Mintzberg, H. The nature of managerial work. New York, Harper and Row, 1973.

Pedler, M.J.; Burgoyne, J.G; Boydell, T.H. <u>A manager's guide to self-development</u>. Maidenhead, McGraw-Hill, 1978.

Shah, I. <u>Learning how to learn</u>. London, Octagon Press, 1980.

SELF-ASSESSMENT AND PLANNING ONE'S OWN FUTURE

2

This chapter concentrates on a number of ways of assessing yourself, as a way of deciding in what ways you want to develop.

However, although self-assessment certainly can provide a most useful first step in your self-development, it is not absolutely essential. Each of us develops anyway, as part of our general life process.

So if you do not yet want to carry out any formal self-assessment, you can still go ahead and accelerate your self-development. You can use some of the methods of chapters 3 to 8 (after all, they are still there, whether or not you have assessed yourself); choose some that appeal to you, or at random. Or do a "mini assessment" by looking through the list of probable outcomes of methods (tables 3 and 4) and select one of those.

You can also concentrate on those activities that are particularly useful in helping you learn to develop from everyday experiences. These will then enable you to make the most out of the developmental opportunities that arise from day to day.

On the other hand, if you would like to have a go at systematic self-assessment, then this chapter can certainly help you.

2.1 The self-assessment process

Self-assessment compared with assessment by others

To some extent we are always assessing ourselves. Every time you feel pleased with something you have done - or dissatisfied with it - then you are in a way assessing yourself.

Often, however, that is as far as it goes. In other words, you do not do anything as a result of your feelings of satisfaction or dissatisfaction. At the same time, the whole process is a bit "hit and miss"; sometimes you are aware how much or how little you have achieved, sometimes you do not notice - or, perhaps, you choose not to notice!

Often, of course, you are forced to look at your performance, or rather someone else forces you. This is usually your boss who, no doubt, from time to time gives you feedback - tells you what he or she thinks of what you have done. Unfortunately, it almost seems a basic human principle that we are much more ready to give negative feedback and adverse criticism than we are to give thanks and praise. Perhaps you should bear this in mind when giving feedback to your subordinates.

Assessment by others - usually your boss - is therefore quite common. There are, however, some very important differences between this and self-assessment. In a sense, they start in the same way with feedback of information. That is, information about you and what you are doing. The difference lies more in the next step.

In conventional assessment, the other person not only gives you the information, but then tells you what to do with it. He or she not only tells you what they think of what you have done, but they also tell you how you must improve, what steps you must now take, what you must do. This is really very much assessment by others.

There is, of course, the approach known as management by objectives (MBO). In theory, this involves you and your boss in a joint negotiation about what you should do, and can therefore be said to be a step towards self-assessment. However, in practice this rarely seems to work out as planned and MBO usually regresses to being a slightly more systematic form of assessment by others.

True self-assessment again starts with you receiving information. This means relatively factual feedback about what you have done, and what has happened as a result. It does not include judgements about what you should have done, or what you ought to do now. So the nature of the information you are getting is different. There are a number of sources of this, some of which are shown in figure 6.

Obviously, other people - including your boss, perhaps - provide one important source of feedback. However, the difference is in what happens with the information. In the case of self-assessment, you decide for yourself what the feedback means, you make your own judgements about yourself, you decide for yourself what to try to change or improve. In all these, you examine what you yourself think, feel and want to do, to refer back to the three inner processes discussed in chapter 1.

However, this is not to say that you ignore other people. Of course not. As has already been mentioned several times, one or more others can be very helpful in discussing things with you, sharing their ideas and experiences, helping you to think about the advantages and disadvantages of your proposed actions. However, in all this they should be helping you to make up your own mind; they should not be giving advice, or instructions, unlike with conventional assessment.

It is not easy to be helpful in this non-directive way; it requires considerable skill. Since you are likely at times to be acting in this role with your colleagues or subordinates, some notes about it are included in chapter 8 under "Working with a speaking partner".

At the same time, you do not live in total isolation from other people and it would therefore be wrong to take no account whatsoever of their feelings and wishes. This would be both selfish and foolish. We will return to this later in this chapter. In the meantime, table 2 summarises some of the important differences between assessment by others and self-assessment.

Table 2. Self-assessment compared with assessment by others

FEATURE	ASSESSMENT BY OTHERS	SELF-ASSESSMENT
Source of feedback information about yourself and your performance.	Other people — especially your boss.	As in figure 6, namely ● a range of other people ● your own analysis of things that happen ("critical incidents") ● other means of self-analysis ● analysis of your whole life, its themes, meaning and purpose ("biography").
Type of feedback information.	Factual and judgemental, with advice and instructions.	Factual, non-judgemental; no advice, no instructions.
Who then decides what the information means, what should be done as a result.	Other people — especially your boss.	Yourself.
Role of others.	Source of information, judgement, advice and instruction.	Source of information. ● Help you to reflect on information and to decide what to do with it. ● Their thinking, feeling and willing to be considered by you when you make your decisions as to what to do.
Timing.	Formally: infrequent, often once a year. Informally: when they feel like it (often when they are displeased with you).	When you are ready. Hopefully, a continuous process.

It will be seen that table 2 also includes a timing factor. Assessment by others is done when they want to — usually either when they are unhappy or dissatisfied with what you have done (informally) or, more formally, at some sort of annual appraisal. Self-assessment, on the other hand, is for when you are ready. It is up to you to decide when to seek feedback, when to analyse your experiences.

Some of the methods of self-assessment described in this chapter and in the appendices tend to be suitable for doing just once, or fairly infrequently. This is particularly true of the questionnaires - although you might find it interesting and helpful to do them again from time to time to see if any differences emerge.

Other methods, especially feedback from others and analysis of critical incidents, can be done often and help you be assess yourself more or less continuously.

In this chapter the various stages in assessing yourself have been explained very systematically. This may give you the impression that the whole thing is a very mechanical process. However, it is important to realise that this need not be the case. As you become skilled at this sort of thing, the separate steps will tend to merge, and again self-assessment will become more continuous, or continuing. Instead of technique, it will become a way of thinking, a way of approaching life.

So, if you like systematic, step-by-step instructions, that is fine. If not, please be tolerant!

Stages in the self-assessment process

Figure 6 presents a summary of the self-assessment process. We will shortly look at each part of this process, but it will be helpful to start with a quick survey.

As has already been discussed, the process starts with you receiving information about yourself and your performance, from various sources. Receiving, collecting and analysing this information leads to an awareness of the main questions and issues facing you.

Figure 6. The self-assessment process

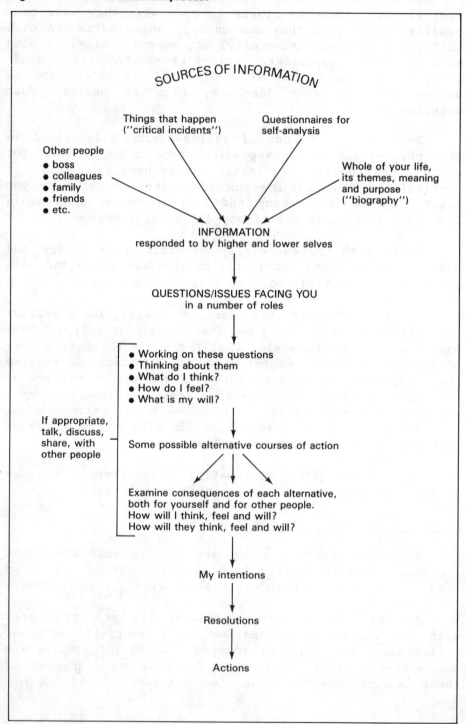

SOURCES OF INFORMATION

Things that happen ("critical incidents")

Questionnaires for self-analysis

Other people
● boss
● colleagues
● family
● friends
● etc.

Whole of your life, its themes, meaning and purpose ("biography")

INFORMATION
responded to by higher and lower selves

QUESTIONS/ISSUES FACING YOU
in a number of roles

● Working on these questions
● Thinking about them
● What do I think?
● How do I feel?
● What is my will?

If appropriate, talk, discuss, share, with other people

Some possible alternative courses of action

Examine consequences of each alternative, both for yourself and for other people.
How will I think, feel and will?
How will they think, feel and will?

My intentions

Resolutions

Actions

Thinking about these questions and issues, often with the help (but not direction) of somebody else, leads you to come up with some possible alternative courses of action: what might you do next? How might you do it?

Each of these possible alternatives can now be evaluated - that is, by examining their consequences, not only for yourself, but for the other people involved. From this, you can make a choice, to which you are committed; this leads, then, to your intentions.

Having quickly surveyed the steps in self-assessment, we will look at each one in a little more detail. Before doing so, however, it will be useful to look at two particular aspects of our inner selves - our higher self and our lower self, as these play a big part in the way we respond to feedback information.

2.2 Our higher and lower selves

Your higher self

In a sense, your higher and lower selves can be said to represent your good and bad qualities. So your higher self - which is part of you - is that part which is honest, courageous, kind, selfless, helpful and so on. It is almost the "angelic" you - so that, at times, we will refer to it as your "angel", which sounds more friendly than "higher self".

Although we all have a higher self, surprisingly, perhaps, many people have difficulty in recognising theirs. These people just cannot see what is good within them. They appear unaware of their strengths and of their lovable features, and if somebody says something nice to them, they become embarrassed, or deny that they have been kind or whatever.

Conversely, other people fall into the trap of self-righteous, proud smugness, and see good qualities in themselves that perhaps are not really there. "Holier than thou" is a good description for such people, as they tend to see nothing but good in themselves, and nothing but bad in others.

Before reading further, it might be helpful for you to write down on a piece of paper what you think are the

45

main features of your higher self; how would you describe your angel? Recognise it, but do not become self-satisfied!

Your lower self

Now let us turn to that which represents your bad qualities - your lower self. Again, we all have a lower self - which we might refer to as our double, or our beast. Your double is that part that contains your less pleasant features - insecurity, pride, envy, hatred, malice, greed, selfishness, and so on.

Since we all have our lower selves, it is again important to recognise these. Denying our unpleasant characteristics is not really going to help us to develop. At the same time, it is important not to let "the beast take over" - that is, we have to avoid becoming so ashamed, guilty and depressed by our lower selves that we lose all confidence and wallow about in fits of self-hatred and self-destruction.

Can you now write down some of the aspects of your lower self or beast? How do you feel about them? Recognise them, but do not let them overpower you! In a sense you can almost be glad about them, because it is these aspects of ourselves that give us something to work on, to improve, as part of our development. In a way we actually need our beasts for us to be able to develop!

In this chapter we are concentrating on looking at the effect your higher and lower selves have on the way you receive feedback, obtain information about yourself and your performance.

In chapter 4 we will come back to these ideas, working with these aspects of yourself - with your angel and your beast - to try to emphasise the one and overcome, or tame the other.

Receiving feedback information

First, let us look at the reaction of your lower self to feedback, which is shown in figure 7.

When your beast is in charge, even positive feedback becomes distorted and channelled in a way that

46

Figure 7. Feedback information received by the lower self

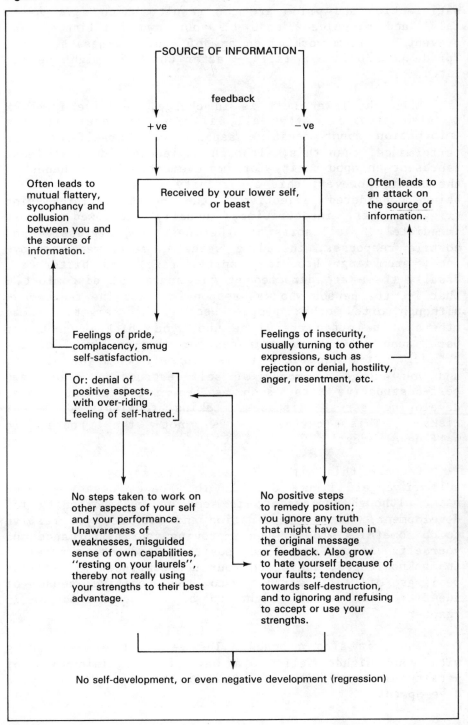

stops it from being helpful. Complacency, self-satisfaction and pride are the result, which give you a false and misguided sense of your own brilliance, and prevent you from working on any of your weaknesses, until "pride goes before a fall" - after which it might be too late.

When the lower self is in charge, negative feedback is also misused. After all, if you are receiving some information about negative aspects of yourself or your performance, then this, although unpleasant, does at least represent an opportunity for improvement. In the hands of the beast, however, this opportunity is lost. Instead of being considered objectively the negative information triggers off insecurities, usually followed almost immediately by all sorts of other negative, aggressive and hostile responses, including sarcasm, resentment, annoyance, grumbling, brooding, spite, rage, and bitterness. Usually these are directed at the source of discomfort - that is, the person who was responsible for the feedback - although often other people become the target. These others quite often are those who, you think, cannot hit back, such as your subordinates, or your children, or the pet dog. At other times it is yourself whom you aim at, and you engage in moods of self-destruction - or even self-destructive acts, such as becoming accident prone, developing stress diseases, taking foolishly dangerous risks. This certainly is not the route to self-development!

Compare this with feedback received by your higher self or angel (figure 8). In this case, negative feedback, although unpleasant, is seen as an opportunity for development. With determination and courage, you resolve to do something, to work on improving your performance and yourself. At the same time, positive feedback is received and acknowledged, adding to your non-complacent, prideless feelings of self worth - to the positive sense of identity, "it is all right to be me", referred to in chapter 1.

There is also a bonus. The very act of responding with your higher self is a way of recognising it, of getting in touch with it. This in itself enhances your development.

Figure 8. Feedback information received by the higher self

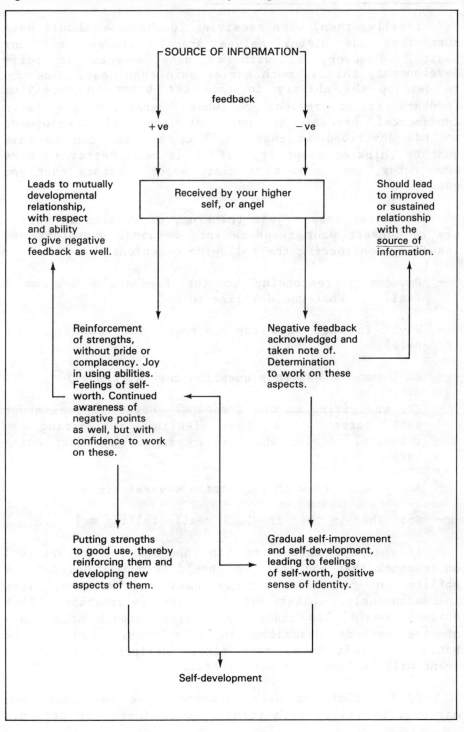

SOURCE OF INFORMATION

feedback

+ve   −ve

Received by your higher self, or angel

Leads to mutually developmental relationship, with respect and ability to give negative feedback as well.

Should lead to improved or sustained relationship with the source of information.

Reinforcement of strengths, without pride or complacency. Joy in using abilities. Feelings of self-worth. Continued awareness of negative points as well, but with confidence to work on these.

Negative feedback acknowledged and taken note of. Determination to work on these aspects.

Putting strengths to good use, thereby reinforcing them and developing new aspects of them.

Gradual self-improvement and self-development, leading to feelings of self-worth, positive sense of identity.

Self-development

49

Receiving feedback constructively

Ideally, then, when receiving feedback we should make sure that our higher selves are in charge, not our beasts! However, as with so many aspects of self-development, this is much easier said than done. One way to develop the ability to tame the beast in receiving feedback is to reflect on what happens. This is a fundamental process in many of the self-development methods described in chapters 3 to 8. You can do this just by thinking about it, but it is much better to make some notes, keep a sort of diary about feedback that you get.

In either case - just thinking, or writing as well - try to convert your feedback into personal questions and issues by considering the following questions:

- How am I responding to the feedback? How am I feeling? What would I like to do?

- Why? In what ways are my angel and beast at work here?

- Am I sure? (Ask this question several times.)

- Who was giving me the feedback? How do I feel about that person? Is that feeling influencing my response? Again, what are my angel and beast doing here?

- Am I sure? (Ask this question several times.)

- So: What is this feedback really telling me?

If you keep reflecting (in thoughts, or in writing) on feedback that you get, you should gradually develop the ability to go through these questions more or less instantaneously, whilst receiving the information. This ability should also gradually develop through using many of the methods described in this book. However, be patient if this takes some time. Reflecting after the event will in itself be very useful.

By the time you have answered these questions, you may well be filled with resolve, with ideas for action.

50

You may even find that one of the effects of merely clarifying this question in itself helps to resolve the issue. There is nothing wrong with that, but do not forget this is still the first part of the self-assessment process of figure 6. So the main thing is to get a sense of what the feedback is saying to you.

2.3 Obtaining information about yourself and your performance

There are many ways of obtaining information about yourself and your performance, and it is clearly impossible to describe all of these in a short publication like this one. Four particularly useful ways have been selected and described in detail in appendices 1 to 4. They are

- feedback from other people;

- things that happen ("critical incidents");

- questionnaires for self-analysis;

- looking at the whole of your life, its themes, meaning and purpose ("biography").

You are not expected to go through each of these ways in turn. In fact, to do it like that would probably be unhelpful, as you would get worn out and bogged down. No. The point of describing a few methods is to give you a choice. We suggest that you briefly look over all the methods, and then choose one that appeals to you most. If you really want to, you can of course do more than one, but it is quite likely that you will want to come back and try another some time later.

Do not forget: these are ways of obtaining information about yourself and your performance, which is only the first part of the self-assessment process (figure 6).

After doing one of the methods, you should then ask yourself, "what is this feedback saying to me? What questions or issues are coming my way?" A method for doing this is described in each case.

51

It might be helpful to give a few examples of what we mean by "issues or questions" - although it is important that you realise that these are only examples. Your own might well be very different. Anyway, here are some:

- my boss: he is asking me "how committed are you to the work of this department?"

- my boss: I want to know how I can get him to let me have more freedom to take initiatives;

- my ambition in life: do I want promotion and material rewards, or a happy family life? Can I have both?

- my ability to sell things: how can I use this to best advantage?

- my poor listening skills: is there anything I can do to improve them?

- my impatience: what can I do about the fact that I get impatient, then angry, when things seem to take longer than I expected?

- my temper: I am often rude to people on the telephone; what can I do about this?

- my wife: she is asking me "is it really necessary for you to go overseas to study for 12 months?"

2.4 Clarifying the questions and issues facing you

If you have gone through all the information-gathering methods described in the appendices, you are probably feeling pretty dizzy and confused! In fact, it is quite likely that you will have concentrated on one or two methods, and that you will come back to the others later.

In any case, you are now at the point where you have quite a lot of information, and a number of questions or issues are facing you, as shown in figure 9.

One of the problems here is that not only might you be suffering from an overload - simply too many issues and

Figure 9. Questions and issues (phase 1)

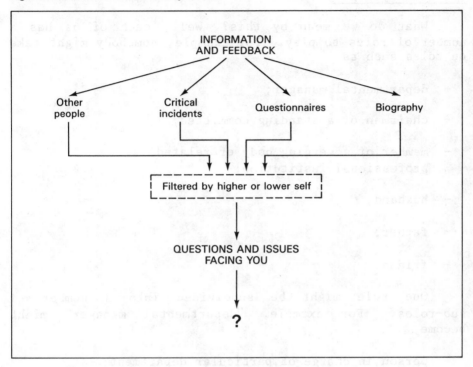

questions to handle at once – but some of these may be in conflict. That is, some could well be contradicting others. Although there is no simple solution to this problem, there are one or two things you can do to make it a bit more manageable.

Firstly, just make a simple list of your key questions and issues, as you now identify them (that is, from whichever of the method(s) you have used). It may be that this simple step will be enough in itself. Looking at your list for a few minutes might be sufficient for one or two priority areas to leap out of the page, as it were, so that you can then concentrate on doing something about those.

However, it is of course quite likely that you will still be finding a lot of confusion in your list of personal questions and issues. In that case, it can be helpful to classify them according to the various roles you adopt in life.

53

The roles you play

What do we mean by this? Well, each of us has a number of roles to play. For example, somebody might take on roles such as

- departmental manager;

- chairman of a standing committee;

- member of governing body or related professional institution;

- husband;

- father;

- friend.

One role might be subdivided into a number of sub-roles. For example, "departmental manager" might become

- person in charge of particular department;

- member of senior management committee;

- friend to certain colleagues.

We are facing a number of different life issues and questions across most of our differing roles. So one way to clarify the possibly bewildering array of such questions is to classify them according to these roles. To do this, a format along the lines of figure 10 is helpful. In the left-hand column, you list the main roles that you play in your life.

You do not have to list all your roles, of course. You might well want to restrict it to those that concern your job - although do not forget the growing importance of recognising the link between job and non-job development, and the need for balance here.

When you have listed your various roles, you can then note the life questions and issues that face you in respect of each one, in the right-hand column of the table.

Figure 10. Roles and questions

Roles you play (job or whole life)	Questions and issues coming your way in respect of each role

Having done this, you should be in a clearer position to choose certain areas and issues to work on. One important difficulty should be mentioned, though. You might well find that the issues in two different roles are more or less diametrically opposed. For example, in your job, you might be being asked to spend more time at the office, or to go overseas on a course, whilst at the same time your children are saying "please spend more time at home".

There is certainly no simple solution to this one! You will have to make a difficult decision. However, there are some ways of analysing these situations in a little more detail, which should help. These ways will now be described.

Identifying alternative courses of action

Now then, we are at the point shown in figure 11. The next step is to explore some of these questions and issues.

The purpose of all this, of course, is to decide on what you are going to do. It is important to distinguish between general wishes (what you would like to do), intentions (what you really are going to do), and first steps (getting started). In order to "jump the gap" between these last two, you also need resolutions - which make a detailed action plan of what you are going to do.

As already mentioned, you can either choose one particular issue, or a number of related ones (including

Figure 11. Questions and issues (phase 2)

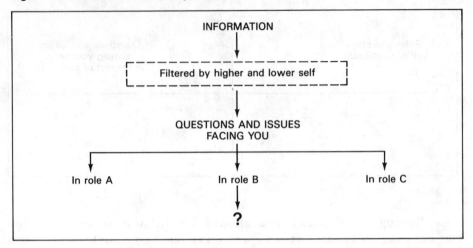

those that clash with each other), or two or three quite separate ones. Do not forget, though, that you can always come back later to look at some more, so it is probably a good idea at this point not to take on too many at once.

On the other hand, at times you will not be able to sort out your priorities until you have in fact examined several in detail. So it is important to keep an eye on the overall picture, examining several, then focussing on certain ones for priority attention.

WISHES:	desired action
INTENTIONS:	motivations to act
RESOLUTIONS:	plan of action
FIRST STEPS:	action

The basic questions are involved yet again here. So, for the various issues you are considering, ask yourself

- what do I think about this?

- how do I feel about it?

- what would I like to do about it?

- what am I prepared to do about it?

- what am I not prepared to do about it?

It is convenient here to look at two types of issue. Examples of the first type might include:

- how can I become a better listener?

- how can I be more assertive?

- how can I improve my physical fitness?

In general, these - which we might term small-scope or narrow-focus issues - tend to focus on one element of your development: of your character, or your skills, or your health, and so on. They are concerned with certain limited aspects of your development.

The second type, on the other hand, are much broader in scope. These involve tackling questions such as:

- I want to set some life goals for the next five years;

- I am dissatisfied with my current job. Should I move to another one, or try to improve things here?

- I have the opportunity to study overseas for a year. Should I take it?

- I am wondering about leaving my current employer and starting up my own business.

Clearly, these types of issue involve much more than just certain specific aspects of your development. They may have a significant influence on your whole life style, and they also affect other people as well.

We can look at the two types of issues separately.

What to do about narrow-focus issues

There are two main ways of dealing with these, as shown in figure 12.

Figure 12. Narrow-focus issues

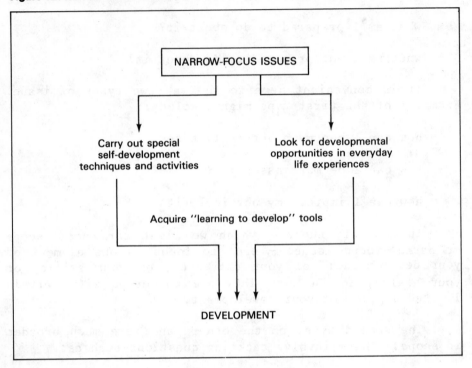

One way, then, is to carry out special self-development techniques and activities, related to the issue or need that you have identified. A number of these are described in chapters 3 to 8, which also give some guidelines on which techniques are particularly suitable for certain types of issue.

However, the other extremely important approach is to use your normal, everyday life experiences as opportunities for development. Since these are happening anyway, let us make the most of them!

Sometimes this can be made easier by translating the issue into action terms.

For example, think about the example of a wish to be more assertive. When? In what circumstances? With whom? Give some examples - when could you practise this? Make it an intention: "I want to be able to tell my boss that I disagree with him". Fine. Then your resolution is that the very next time you disagree, you will tell him so. And when you do tell him, you have taken your first step.

Or take another example. "I want to listen to my immediate subordinate more. At present I ignore what he says." Fine. Then resolve to do it - the very next time he comes to talk to you. And when he does - take your first step.

Of course, it is all very well to say "Fine - then do it". Obviously it is not as easy as that! But this can show you the opportunities that exist. Very probably, when the opportunity actually arrives, you will not do as well as you would have liked. Very well - use that as part of the learning experience. Turn it into a critical incident, and analyse it as already described earlier in this chapter. Learn from the failure - or success.

What to do about broader-focus issues

These questions, of course, are somewhat different from the narrow-focus ones. For example, there is no simple exercise or activity that will tell you whether or not you should change your job. There are, though, a number of things you can do to help you with these broader issues.

If you have not done it already, you will probably find that going through the biography process (appendix 4) will be helpful. This can clarify the main questions facing you, and can also give insights into your main life-themes, which can play an important part in making an important life decision.

With these bigger questions, you will almost certainly recognise several alternative answers or solutions. For example, suppose you are thinking about changing your job. Various alternatives could include:

- no; stay where I am and try to make things better here;

- yes; look for an internal transfer;

- yes; look for a job in another organisation.

At this stage, it is useful to take each alternative in turn, and examine it very carefully. First, note all the obvious advantages and disadvantages, in terms of outcomes, ease or difficulty in carrying it out, likelihood of success or failure. Since we are trying to prevent self-development from being selfish, you should also look at each from the point of view of the other people who are likely to be affected. What are the good and bad points as far as they are concerned?

Then take each one in turn again. Imagine that it is now a time in the future, after you carried out that particular choice. So, you have chosen that one, and put it into action.

Now imagine to yourself, what is happening? Who are all the people involved? What is going on? What am I doing? What are all the other people doing? What am I thinking? How am I feeling? What am I wanting to do? (All this in your imagination, in the future, as a result of your choice.)

What are the other people thinking? How are they feeling? What are they wanting to do?

Put as much detail into this imagination as you possibly can. Really try to feel, hear, smell, touch, as well as see what is happening.

Doing this imaginative exercise will help you to get a clearer impression of the features of each choice. It breathes life into your list of advantages and disadvantages, making them more meaningful, more real.

Having said that, a new complication might now emerge. It is quite likely that you will still be faced with some conflicts amongst the choices. For example, you might realise that choice A will lead to some people being happy, others less so. Choice B affects different people. Choice C requires approval or sanction by your employer. Which do you choose? Only you can decide. In the end, you have to make the difficult choice. But ...

- you do this after examining the alternatives carefully; you have followed through the consequences for everybody involved, and have taken these into account along with your own wishes; therefore you are taking a morally responsible decision;

- this may help you to talk with those people; after all, your imagination of their reactions might be wrong; in any case, if they are so likely to be affected, do not they have the right to be consulted?

- having considered these things consciously, perhaps you will be in a better position to "brief" people as to what you want to do; if it is something that will upset them, can you now think of ways of telling them that will minimise their upset?

2.5 A self-development plan

Particularly with these broader issues, it is recommended that you draw up an actual self-development plan. An extensive development programme involves a whole host of factors (e.g. time, other people, finance, other resources), and it is useful to identify these so as to get a picture of all the implications.

Of course, self-development cannot always be expected to follow a neat path. None the less, we suggest that you prepare a plan which includes:

- overall goal of your programme;

- sub-goals;

- dates by which you hope to achieve these;

- other people involved, and the nature of their involvement;

- other resources necessary.

You should also discuss the plan with those involved - in particular with your employer, and, perhaps, with your spouse and family.

It is important to recognise, too, that it is <u>your</u> <u>plan</u>, and you are responsible. It is no use waiting for someone to come along and make you a "development offer". <u>You</u> have to take the initiative, be pro-active!

2.6 <u>Suggestions for further reading</u>

Ferrucci, P. <u>What we may be</u>. Wellingborough, Turnstone, 1982.

Hoslett, S.D. "Self-analysis: Benchmarks for development", <u>American Management Association Report No. 63</u>, 1961.

Lievegoed, B. <u>Phases</u>. London, Rudolf Steiner Press, 1979.

Manpower Services Commission: <u>Management self-development manual</u>. Sheffield, Manpower Services Commission, 1983.

Sheehy, G. <u>Passages: Predictable crises of adult life</u>. New York, Bantam, 1977.

Woodcock, M.; Francis, D. <u>The unblocked manager</u>. Aldershot, Gower, 1982.

METHODS AND RESOURCES
FOR SELF-DEVELOPMENT

3

3.1 Selecting methods and resources

In chapters 4 to 8 we present brief descriptions of methods, techniques or resources for self-development. In each case the method is discussed in terms of what it involves, how you might set about it, and what some of the outcomes or effects are likely to be.

This last aspect - possible outcomes or effects poses a bit of a problem. First, they are only possible outcomes; so much depends on your commitment and on how hard you yourself are prepared to work at it.

Perhaps you have seen advertisements in newspapers for special books, or equipment, that are "guaranteed to bring success without trying". Well, sorry, but that is not the case here. (Nor, we suspect, is it really true with most of those advertisements!)

No. As already described in chapter 1, self-development requires hard work. Certainly there are a number of methods, techniques, tools and resources that can be of undoubted value. But this value will only be realised if you are prepared to make them work.

Indeed, we might go so far as to formulate a rule, namely that:

THE MORE I PUT INTO USING THESE METHODS,

THE MORE I WILL GET OUT.

People often ask of a book or a course "What will I get out of this?" Answer: "You will get out of it according to how much you put into it".

You should also remember that most of the methods need time to work. It is no use doing them once, and then expecting good results.

For example, you would not expect to become physically fit just by going for one five-mile run. However, if you gradually built up to it and then ran five miles every day, the benefits would be most marked. So it is with these activities. Do not expect too much to start with – there are no instant developments! Start gradually, with one or two methods, and keep doing them regularly. Later on, introduce some others to your programme.

Some of the activities should ideally be done every day. Others regularly, but less frequently – say once a week or month. And there are some that are only really useful on specific occasions, when something has happened that makes them particularly relevant.

In this chapter, figure 13 provides a summary of the methods, which gives some indication of the most likely benefits of each in terms of the qualities and skills required for self-development. It then does the same, for the qualities of an effective manager and of a developed person.

If possible, then, you should try to plan your self-development programme around a regular pattern of carrying out certain activities – just a few to start with. Setting aside a particular time of day will be especially helpful, or a particular day of the week for less frequent activities. (One on one day, a different one the next day, perhaps.)

So, where do you start? Well, this will depend a lot on the personal issue you want to work on. If you have gone through one or more of the self-assessment activities from chapter 2, you will probably have quite a good idea as to what this issue is. Figure 13 will help here.

Alternatively, you might prefer just to choose a method because it looks interesting. There is certainly no harm in that; far from it.

Figure 13. Summary table of self-development methods

METHODS AND ACTIVITIES	CHAPTER	CHARACTERISTICS OF A DEVELOPED PERSON (ART OF MANAGEMENT)												QUALITIES OF AN EFFECTIVE MANAGER (SCIENCE OF MANAGEMENT)											TOOLS FOR LEARNING TO DEVELOP FROM EVERYDAY WORK AND LIFE EXPERIENCE	QUALITIES NEEDED FOR SELF-DEVELOPMENT				SKILLS REQUIRED FOR SELF-DEVELOPMENT					
		HEALTH			SKILLS			ACTION			IDENTITY																			INITIATING	RESPONDING	LOOKING FORWARD	LOOKING BACK	THEORISING	PRACTICAL MOVEMENT
		MENTAL HEALTH	EMOTIONAL HEALTH	PHYSICAL HEALTH	MENTAL SKILLS	EXPRESSIVE AND SOCIAL SKILLS	PHYSICAL SKILLS	MAKING DECISIONS	KEEPING GOING	TAKING INITIATIVES	SELF-KNOWLEDGE	FEELING ABOUT SELF	PURPOSE IN LIFE	COMMAND OF BASIC FACTS	RELEVANT PROFESSIONAL KNOWLEDGE	SENSITIVITY TO EVENTS	DECISION MAKING	SOCIAL SKILLS	EMOTIONAL RESILIENCE	PROACTIVITY	CREATIVITY	MENTAL AGILITY	BALANCED LEARNING HABITS	SELF-KNOWLEDGE		COURAGE	OPENNESS	FAITH	HOPE						

(The following matrix indicates, with dots, which qualities, characteristics and skills each method develops.)

#	Method and activity	Chapter
1	PERSONAL JOURNAL	4
2	BACKWARDS REVIEW	4
3	REFLECTING ON THINGS THAT HAPPEN	4
4	LISTENING TO YOUR INNER SELF AND SELF-COUNSELLING; INTUITION	4
5	COURAGE TO TRY OUT NEW THINGS	4
6	EXPERIMENTING WITH NEW BEHAVIOURS	4
7	IMPROVING YOUR WILL-POWER	4
8	KEEPING AN OPEN MIND	4
9	WORKING WITH YOUR HIGHER AND LOWER SELVES	4
10	READING	5
11	NOTE TAKING	5
12	REPERTORY GRID	5
13	WAYS OF REMEMBERING THINGS	5
14	IMPROVING YOUR ABILITY TO THINK LOGICALLY	5
15	COURSES, INCLUDING CORRESPONDENCE	6
16	PACKAGES AND PROGRAMMED LEARNING	6
17	SPECIAL PROJECTS	6
18	JOINING ASSOCIATIONS AND PROFESSIONAL BODIES	6
19	WRITING FOR JOURNALS	6
20	TEACHING AND TRAINING OTHERS	6
21	WORKING WITH PHYSICAL FITNESS, RELAXATION AND MEDITATION	7
22	WORKING WITH YOUR SIZE, SHAPE AND APPEARANCE	7
23	WORKING WITH PEOPLE WHO ARE DIFFERENT	7
24	WORKING WITH YOUR TEMPERAMENTS	7
25	WORKING WITH YOUR MANAGERIAL STYLE	7
26	WORKING WITH A SPEAKING PARTNER	8
27	GROUP APPROACHES	8

However you start, do remember again that "time will tell". Instant results should not be expected!

In figure 13, and the descriptions in the following chapters, an attempt has been made to arrange the methods and resources in particular clusters.

First come some fundamental activities that can form the basic underpinning of your whole self-development programme (chapter 4). As well as leading to some of the general developmental outcomes, you will see from figure 13 that these also help with the qualities and skills required for development.

Chapter 5 then concentrates on ways of improving your logical, rational thinking. Chapter 6 looks at some other opportunities for self-development that you can use, and then chapter 7 concentrates on physical fitness and on certain specific aspects of knowing yourself. Finally, chapter 8 describes another very important aspect - namely working with other people on your self-development.

Perhaps we should emphasise that we are not saying that you should attempt all the activities and methods. Not only would this simply not be feasible, but you would also be overloading yourself with development! You would probably then suffer from some sort of nervous strain or collapse.

We are presenting quite a large number of methods so that you have a choice. There are plenty of things to choose from when planning your development programme, either according to your self-assessment, or depending on which ones just seem to appeal to you. Since self-development is a continuous, lifelong process, the activities that you do not choose in the first instance will still be there later when you do need them.

3.2 Suggestions for further reading

You might like to acquire the following publications, which also provide complete packages of self-development materials and exercises.

Austin, C.F. Management's self-inflicted wounds. New York, Holt, Rinehart and Winston, 1966.

66

Manpower Services Commission: Management self-development manual. Sheffield, Manpower Services Commission, 1983.

Pedler, M.J.; Burgoyne, J.G.; Boydell, T.H. A manager's guide to self-development. Maidenhead, McGraw Hill, 1978.

Woodcock, M.; Francis, D. The unblocked manager. Aldershot, Gower, 1982.

For additional reading on a number of methods for self-development, see

Boydell, T.H.; Pedler, M.J. (eds). Management self-development concepts and practices. Aldershot, Gower, 1981.

SOME FUNDAMENTAL METHODS

4

In this chapter we present nine basic methods. As well as leading to a variety of general developmental outcomes, they also are particularly useful for working on the qualities and skills required for development, as discussed in chapter 2. The methods are:

(1) personal journal;

(2) backwards review;

(3) reflecting on things that happen;

(4) listening to your inner self,
    self-counselling, intuition;

(5) courage to try out new things;

(6) experimenting with new behaviour;

(7) improving your will-power;

(8) keeping an open mind;

(9) working with your higher
    and lower selves.

4.1 Method 1: Personal journal

It can be very useful indeed to keep a personal journal, or self-development diary. You can use such a journal in a number of ways. For example, you can:

- keep a diary of the main events of the day, particularly as they relate to your self-development;

- write down answers and/or scores from self-analysis questionnaires (such as those in the appendices);

- use it to do the various pencil and paper exercises in this chapter;

- record any thoughts that suddenly come to you;

- copy out short passages from books or newspapers; poems; small sketches;

- use it for your incident diary (see section 4.3).

How you organise your journal is up to you. You might want to keep it in a notebook of some sort (you can often find, these days, particularly nice ones, with most attractive covers). Or you might prefer a loose-leaf system, which would allow you to divide it up into sections - one for diary entries, another for critical incidents, another for pencil and paper exercises, and so on.

As you make entries in your journal, this will in itself help you to focus on your development, to concentrate on what is happening. From time to time you can look back at it, looking for patterns, themes, trends, progress.

Highly recommended. Almost essential.

4.2 Method 2: Backwards review

This is a way of regularly reflecting on what you have been doing.

It is easy to explain. At the end of each day, you go over, in your imagination, everything that has happened. You do this in reverse order. That is, you start with the most recent thing you did and work back through the day, until you reach the point where you woke up that morning.

It is important to try to do more than merely make a mental list of what you did. Try to imagine it; observe yourself, in your imagination, doing the various things. Witness what you were thinking, how you were feeling, what you wanted to do and actually did. See the environment, the other people involved. Hear what people said, what other noises were made. Feel the warmth. Smell any smells. Thus, become aware of everything that was going on, and of how various elements affected each other.

Although it sounds simple enough, this activity is surprisingly difficult. It is very easy to let your mind wander off on to something else. It is also rather a good way of falling asleep very rapidly! So it is preferable to do it sitting up, before actually going to bed.

If you practise this regularly, you will find that not only does it provide insights about yourself, how you behave, and why, but it will also help to develop your powers of logical thinking. The need to force yourself as it were, "against the tide" of what actually happened, sharpens up your thinking abilities; it will also probably help to improve your memory.

Another benefit accrues from practising this regularly. You will almost certainly find that to do so requires quite a high degree of self-discipline, of effort. Exercising this self-discipline will also help to develop your will-power (see also method 7).

4.3 Method 3: Reflecting on things that happen

You will recall that in chapter 1 we discussed "the development cycle" - that is, the process of making sense of experiences, hence learning and developing (figure 3).

One of the steps in that process involves thinking about the experience, reflecting on what happened. In this section we will describe two techniques for helping with this reflection.

Incident diary

In some ways this is similar to the record of critical incidents that is used as one of the self-assessment methods discussed in the appendices. However, rather than taking specific, important things that had happened to you sometime in the past, the incident diary is a more continuous, ongoing thing, the purpose of which is to help you learn from a stream of experiences.

There are various types of incident diary. For example, your diary can focus on the following issues:

- the main things that happen each day;

- conflicts: recording incidents and experiences that involved you in a conflict with somebody or something;

- successes: recording incidents and experiences that were, you feel, successes;

- failures: this time you record failure experiences;

- decisions: you record important decisions that you make;

- nice things: concentrates on nice things that are said to you, or done for or to you;

- will-power: when you did and did not exercise will-power (see also method 7);

- open-mindedness: when you were open-minded and also when you were closed-minded, prejudiced (see also method 8);

- feelings: a record of any strong feelings that you get.

Whichever issues you record, try to look out for the main points, by noting:

- what happened;

- what you thought;

- how you felt;

- what you wanted to do, and actually did do;

- who else was involved;

- what you think they thought, felt, wanted to do, did do.

When you have been keeping a diary for some time, go back over what you have been writing and look to see if any patterns or themes emerge. Can you learn from what the various other involved people have done?

You can, if you wish, keep your diary as part of your personal journal (method 1). However, as there will probably be lots of entries in that, covering a range of topics, it may be better to have a separate notebook for the specialised incident diary — although you could combine the two by starting the diary from the back of the journal, working with it upside down.

Write a story

This method combines detailed writing with imaginative reviewing. You can do it either after an imaginative, visual backwards review, or you can go straight into it, on its own.

Again, you concentrate on a particular experience or happening. This time, though, you write about it as though you were writing a story, or novel.

You use the third person to describe all the characters, including yourself. So, instead of writing "I felt very excited at this", you write "Tom felt very excited at this".

Similarly with all the other characters. Having to describe what they thought, felt and wanted to do will probably make you realise that in fact you do not know; the best you can do is to make a guess, based on various clues.

(Afterwards, of course, you could go and check out with them how they were in fact responding.)

In this way, you will be helped to look at yourself objectively, in a way that hopefully allows you to recognise your thoughts, feelings and intentions whilst remaining controlled, in equilibrium.

4.4 Method 4: Listening to your inner self and self-counselling; the development of intuition

As well as our conscious thoughts and ideas, that is, the ones we are aware of, we all have a subconscious mind. This is full of excellent ideas, knowledge, advice on what to do and not to do and feedback information to ourselves. It is the source of what is often referred to as "intuition".

Unfortunately, however, by its very nature (subconscious means that we are not normally aware of it) we usually do not hear this stream of information. Although we each have a personal "inner voice" that is trying to help us, we do not listen to it.

The seven techniques described in this section are designed to help us to hear our guardian "inner voice". When would these techniques be particularly useful? More or less all the time, but especially

- when faced with a difficult decision;

- when having to make a painful choice between alternatives;

- when everything seems to be going wrong, your life is in a bit of a mess, and you do not know which way to turn;

- when you are about to do or say something that might have quite a significant effect (for better or worse) on yourself and/or other people. In this case, your inner voice might be able to tell you whether or not this is the right thing to do; or it might help you realise that there is in fact a better way of doing it;

- when you are frightened or worried, you can call on your inner self to give you courage (see also method 5).

The seven techniques are

(a) letting go of the problem;

(b) carrying a notebook;

(c) checking your motives;

(d) listening to your own thinking, feeling and willing;

(e) talking with yourself;

(f) praying;

(g) using pauses and silences.

One important point should be made here — do not forget we all have a higher and lower inner self. You need to be on the look out to notice which one you are hearing! (See also method 9, for more on this.)

(a) Letting go of the problem

This technique is particularly useful when faced with what we might call "creative" problems. That is, when you are trying to find new ways of doing something; or are looking for the right way to explain something; or you are seeking new ideas.

Often when we are working on such a problem we churn it over and over in our head, until in the end we just "cannot think straight". We get confused, frustrated, anxious, perhaps with a headache, backache, or some other physical symptom. In this state, the last thing we are likely to do is to come up with something creative. The thing to do, then, is to let go of the problem, forget about it.

Easier said than done, perhaps. However, if you occupy yourself with something else, you will probably be able to forget it for a time. So go and get on with another task altogether. Or go for a walk; visit a friend; do something in the garden; watch or play football, go for a swim, or something else physical; play cards, chess, or similar type of game popular in your own country; or do some hobby work.

75

Taking your mind off the problem will not only relax you (see also method 21), but, more important as far as this section is concerned, it will quieten down your conscious mind so that your subconscious, or inner voice, can get through. Surprisingly often, when doing something different or relaxing, you suddenly get a flash of insight; you suddenly realise what you must do, or how to solve the problem, or just what is needed.

(b) Carrying a notebook

This is in many ways a continuation of letting go. Since good ideas, solutions, things you have realised or remembered you have to do, questions you want to find answers to, often come "out of the blue" in the way just described, it helps if you have a way of capturing them.

A small notebook or notepad is most useful for this. If you carry it with you wherever you can, you will then be able to note down, quickly and simply, all the ideas and so on that suddenly arrive in this way.

(c) Checking your motives

This one is useful when making a decision, choosing an alternative, or just before actually doing something important. Quite simply, it involves you asking yourself "Why am I doing this?"; or "What am I really trying to do?"

For example, suppose you are about to talk to a subordinate who has made a mess of something - you are going to give him negative feedback. Before doing so, ask "Why am I doing this?". There may be various reasons. A positive one would be because you want to help that person, so that they can do better next time. All too often, though, we realise we are doing it to punish, or to get revenge for something someone else has done to us ("so I will jolly well pass on my punishment to the next one down the line"), or to avoid tackling another problem. This is when your lower self is in control.

You can still go ahead, of course, and punish, get revenge, release your own anger and frustration, or whatever it is. But at least you will now be aware of what you are doing; it will be done consciously. On the other

76

hand, your higher self may well come into play and you will then modify your approach to the task in hand.

The same applies when you are making a difficult decision, or are faced with a painful choice. Asking yourself "Why am I involved in this?", or "What am I really trying to do?", may help you to realise your motives, which in turn can lead you to get quite a different perspective on the situation.

(d) Listening to your own thinking, feeling and willing

This is really an extended version of checking your motives. It involves asking yourself questions like those shown in table 3.

(e) Talking with yourself

Although sometimes said to be a sign of madness, talking with yourself can in fact be a good way of getting in touch with your inner voice.

In effect, you have to act as your own speaking partner (method 26). This requires you to play two parts - your normal self (or conscious self), and your inner voice (or subconscious self).

Your normal self starts off by explaining the problem, issue or situation confronting you. Your inner voice personality listens and then responds, using the same methods as are described in chapter 8. That is, your inner voice asks you questions, supports, challenges, and so on.

If you can overcome your initial embarrassment, it is best if you do this out loud.

Some people find it easier to write the conversation rather than speak it. This does have the advantage of providing you with a record of what was said, but most people find it much easier to talk than to write.

(f) Praying

Where does your inner voice come from? Many people would say that it is purely an internal reflection of what you know already, deep in your subconscious.

77

Table 3. Listening to yourself

POSTURE	• How am I sitting? Am I slumped, or upright?
	• Am I attending? Or am I distracting myself by fiddling, gazing around, allowing my attention to be diverted?
	• How is my breathing? Rapid and shallow? Or deep and regular?
THINKING, FEELING AND WILLING	• What am I thinking? Why? What effects are these thoughts having?
	• How am I feeling? Why? What effects are these feelings having?
	• What would I like to do? Why? What effect is this wish having?
	• What am I prepared to do? Why?
	• What am I not prepared to do? Why?
	• What will be the effects of doing or not doing these things?
INNER VOICE	• Am I listening to my inner voice; or am I blocking it? How? Why?
	• How many inner voices can I hear?
	• What are my inner voice(s) telling me? Why? What is their motivation?
	• So what? What do I think, feel and want to do as a result of what my inner voice(s) are telling me?

However, quite a different view can be taken if you have religious and spiritual beliefs that include the existence of some form of God. If so, you might like to identify your inner voice as being the route by which you receive "messages" from your God.

In this case, of course, prayer becomes a means of making contact with your inner voice. In this way, "listening to yourself" becomes "listening to what your God is telling you".

(g) Using pauses and silences

All too often we make it very difficult, if not impossible, to hear our inner voices, wherever they come from, by filling our lives with noise, distraction, activity and busyness. Whichever method we use to listen to our inner voice, it helps therefore if we can create space for it by cutting out most of the noise and distraction.

One way to do this is to pause before actually doing something, before taking action. There is an old saying about "counting up to ten" when you are feeling angry with somebody, the idea being that by doing this you will be able to control yourself. Pausing before action is really the same sort of thing. During the pause - or short silence, if it is a pause in a conversation or discussion - try to tune in to yourself, tune in to your inner voice. Listen to your thinking, feeling and willing. Check your motives. Make sure that you really do want to do whatever it is you are about to do and that you are not merely acting on an impulse that you will regret later.

You will find this quite difficult. We are so used to reacting instantly, to "jumping to it", that it is difficult to break the habit. However, if you can learn to do so, and hence to make sure you are doing what you really want to, when you are really ready, the effects can be most beneficial.

As well as pausing ("look before you leap") before action, longer periods of silence can be very productive.

If you can find a few quiet minutes, use them to listen to yourself, either using one or other of the methods described in this section, or just remaining silent. Sit or lie down comfortably and just stay quiet. Messages from inside may then start to arrive - although at first they may be confusing, and may not seem to relate to anything in particular. Our subconscious often has to get a lot off its chest to start with.

The use of silences in this way leads into the area of meditation, which is discussed later (chapter 7). Particularly relevant is the meditation on silence.

4.5   Method 5: Courage to try out new things

As already described, one of the qualities needed for self-development is courage, without which it is often difficult to try out new things and take initiatives.

Other people as a source of courage

It is not always easy to develop such courage. One way is by sharing your issues and concerns with others - either in pairs (i.e. with a speaking partner, see method 26), or in a group (method 27).

Indeed, giving courage and determination can be one of the main effects of working in a group. Hearing other people's problems, and seeing the way in which they are tackling them can be very inspiring.

Furthermore, there is a particular approach, either in pairs or in a group, that can lead to courage and determination to do something. This involves each member making a public statement (i.e. to the rest of the group) in which you declare what you are going to do, or try out, before the next meeting.

Then, at the start of the next meeting, each of you reports back on what you have done.

You will probably find that, during the time between the meetings, the knowledge that you are going to have to report back, to account for yourself, is quite a spur to action! "I dare not go back and admit that I have done nothing". At the same time, the knowledge that the group (or your partner), is with you mentally, if not physically, when doing whatever it is, can also be very supportive, and can help you to overcome your fear or reluctance.

Examining the worst that could happen

Another way of generating courage is to examine the worst that could happen as a result of your action.

Suppose you are wanting to do something, but it appears risky; you are in some ways frightened. Frightened of what? It could be fear of

- appearing stupid;

- making a fool of yourself;

- provoking a row with somebody;

- losing a friendship;

- destroying some equipment;

- ruining a lot of previous hard work.

Often, though, these and similar fears lurk in our minds, without much substance. So it can be very helpful to examine them in more detail.

Take whatever it is that you would like to do, or change. Then imagine that you are going it, and that you are succeeding. It is going extremely well. Try to observe what you are thinking, feeling and wanting to do. Also, who else is involved? What are they thinking, feeling and willing as a result of your successful achievement?

When you have done that, repeat the exercise, but this time imagine that everything has gone badly. Your worst fears have come true! What is that like, what is happening, how are you and everybody else thinking, feeling and willing?

It may be that the effect of this is to reinforce your fears. You decide not to do anything. But at least this is now a conscious decision, as the result of examining the issue carefully, rather than due to some vague, half-recognised subconscious fear.

81

On the other hand, there is a good chance that examining it in this way will show you that the worst that can happen - although not very nice - really is not too awful after all. It is hardly the end of the world! In this case, you might well then find enough courage and will to act.

Inspiration from symbols of courage

Many people gain courage from some symbol that they find personally meaningful.

For example, many gain courage from symbols associated with their particular religious beliefs. These may indeed be symbols as such (e.g. the cross, the crescent), or they may be more than that, in the form of a particular God, Saint, or sacred personality.

Others gain this type of inspiration by thinking of popular folk heroes, either from ancient traditions and myths, or from more recent history. Religious or political martyrs can be referred to as well.

Finally, you can always refer to your inner self, or, more particularly, your higher self (method 9). "Come on Tom, pull yourself together and get on with it", can be a surprisingly powerful order to yourself!

Incidentally, there are also a few exercises to help develop your will-power, which can also affect your courage and determination (method 7).

4.6 Method 6: Experimenting with new behaviours

A good way of developing is to set out, quite consciously, to try new ways of doing things.

Indeed, we might almost say that since development by its very nature, involves changing, then unless you are prepared to try out new things then you will not develop.

Most of the changes or new behaviours that you will want to try will arise as a result of other developmental activities. For example, the self-assessment methods of chapter 2 will probably lead you to want to change various aspects of your behaviour, and to try new ways of doing things.

82

The same may be said of many of the other activities. Studying entries in your personal journal (method 1) may show various patterns or habits that you would like to alter; reviewing past events (method 2) may have here the same effect. Feedback from your speaking partner (method 26) might tell you about something you would like to do differently. And so on.

You can also get ideas about new ways of trying things by remaining open to other people's ideas (method 8).

However, it is not just enough to know what you want to change, or to do differently. You need both the will to do it, and a degree of courage.

We have already looked at some ways of trying to develop courage (method 5). Later there is a discussion on ways of trying to improve your will-power (method 7). To some extent, though, you can work on courage, will-power, and the ability to try new things, all at the same time. This involves practising making changes - changes which in themselves do not appear to be particularly significant.

For example, you can

- change your style of clothes, or part of them. If you normally wear something rather formal, start being informal; or vice versa;

- try eating completely different types of food - preferably things you have never eaten before;

- list a few situations you would normally avoid, and then deliberately put yourself in one of them;

- change your means of travel to work (e.g. public transport instead of car; walk instead of public transport);

- change the types of book you read, or radio programme you listen to, or TV show you watch;

- try to talk to at least one complete stranger every day.

In your diary (method 2) you can focus on change. Each day, you record at least one thing you have done differently. In each case, of course, ask yourself what you were thinking, how you were feeling, what you wanted to do and what you actually did do.

In this way, you will gradually find that you are developing the ability to make changes, so that you will find it easier to make the more significant ones that are to be part of your self-development programme.

4.7   Method 7: Improving your will-power

A strong will-power is both something that is needed for self-development, and something that will grow as a result of it. Will-power is strengthened by using it. So, a bit like the chicken and the egg, which comes first?

Insights into your will-power

Think carefully about your will. When is it strong? When is it weak? Do any patterns emerge? Is it affected by other people? Who? By time of day? By pressures of work? By tiredness? Or what?

You might get further insights into this if in your diary you focus on occasions when your will is strong, and on those when it is weak.

If patterns and characteristics of your will-power do not emerge quite readily, you can use the repertory grid technique (method 12) for a more systematic analysis. You would use the occasions when your will is strong, and when it is weak, as the examples along the top of the grid chart (figure 14).

Activities in this book as a means of improving your will-power

Some of the exercises in this book - those that involve regular activity - require will-power. To do something according to a set programme requires effort of the will.

Conversely, if you do succeed in sticking to those regular activities, you will in fact be improving your will-power. It is a positive circle, as in figure 14.

Figure 14. Will-power improvement cycle

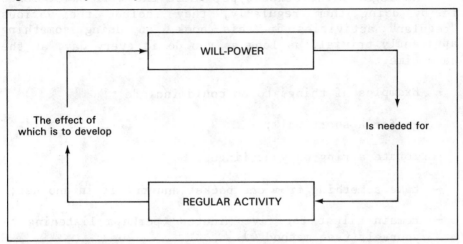

Although most of the book's activities can be done on a regular basis, this applies to some more than others. Particularly suitable ones include the backwards review (method 2), reflecting on things that happen (method 3), and meditation (method 21).

Other activities for developing will-power

You can also try out other ways of developing your will-power. These are very simple, and can usually be done as part of your everyday life. Some of them require an effort of will just to do. Others in themselves require virtually no effort - exercising your will comes in when you try to do them every day.

Here are some examples of the first type - that is, those that require quite a degree of will-power to do in the first place:

- do not say something that you are tempted to say;

- if you want to do something immediately - postpone it;

- if you want to postpone something - do it now;

- make one of the changes suggested in method 6;

- do something that you are frightened of (see also method 5 on courage).

As regards the other type, where the will-power comes in by doing them regularly, they include the various "regular" activities in this book, on doing something apparently trivial, as long as you do it every day, at the same time.

Examples of things to do could include

- go for a short walk;

- rotate a ring on your finger;

- take something from one pocket and put it in another;

- remain silent for five minutes (perhaps listening to yourself (see method 4).

These, of course, are all structured, or somewhat artificial or contrived. You can always be on the lookout for opportunities to practise using your will-power. For example, when you want to do something, but feel "I cannot be bothered". Or conversely, when you do not want to, but somehow can hardly stop yourself. These present perfect opportunities to let your will-power have a go, and hence strengthen itself.

4.8 Method 8: Keeping an open mind

This is a bit like will-power, in that it is both an outcome and a requirement of self-development. Again, the more you practise it, the more it develops.

Ordinary life is full of opportunities for practising open-mindedness. Basically it is a question of coming to every situation, listening to every person, without prejudice or prejudgement. This is easier said than done, of course.

Are you open- or closed-minded?

It might help if you start by understanding a bit more about your own level of open-mindedness. To do this, try to remember a number of situations in which you have been presented with something that you strongly disagree with. Often this will have involved you in listening and talking with someone whose opinions and views you do not share. Other examples would include reading (books, journals, newspapers); listening to radio or television - especially on political topics.

If you cannot recall any, make a start by noting down such situations over a period of a week or two in your diary. You can also recall or record times when you heard something that you did agree strongly with. Having our own favourite theories and prejudices confirmed is another example of closed-mindedness. Being easily swayed by someone else, without proper thought, shows you are too open-minded.

Having collected or recalled a number of such incidents, look over them. Look for any patterns or themes that might emerge. When are you relatively open-minded? When are you closed-minded? Are certain people involved in each? Who? Why?

These themes and patterns will probably emerge fairly readily. If you want to do a more systematic analysis, the repertory grid (method 12) would be most appropriate, using "times when I strongly disagreed or strongly agreed" as the examples along the top of the repertory grid chart (figure 18).

What sort of characteristics of closed-minded situations might emerge? Clearly, this depends a lot on you, but they might include

- when you dislike the person involved, or think they are stupid;

- when you like the person a lot, or think they are clever, or expert, (too open-minded, or gullible);

- when your basic beliefs are challenged;

- when you have often disagreed with the other person before, so you assume he or she is talking nonsense this time;

- when what is said seems to show that something you have worked hard at is no longer useful or valuable;

- when what is being suggested might cause you a lot of

administrative difficulties, or problems with your boss;

- when it looks as though it will involve you in a lot of extra work, or in an unacceptable risk;

- when it makes you feel unnecessary, redundant; it devalues you, your ideas, your role;

- when it causes you to lose face, to backtrack on previously stated ideas or beliefs;

- because you just do not like the idea that someone else may be right and you may be wrong;

- when it confirms your own views and criticises those of people who disagree with you (too open-minded, or gullible);

- when it seems to present a nice, simple, safe solution (too open-minded, or gullible).

An exercise to develop open-mindedness

A specific exercise to develop open-mindedness might be called "devil's advocate". Quite simply, it involves choosing an issue on which you have strong views, and then imagining that you have to present "the case for the opposition".

That is, you find as many points as possible that support the opposing view, and challenge your own. To do so will probably also require quite a lot of will-power.

Just finding these points will in itself probably help you to be more open-minded, to see more than one point of view. You can, if you wish, reinforce this by writing an essay which praises the opposite case, as well as your own.

Alternatively, this can be a good exercise to do with a partner. Ideally you should choose someone who disagrees with you, or find a topic on which you disagree. Each then prepares the case for the opposition, and talks about it with the other. That is, you have to argue for the opinions that you do not in fact hold.

Open-mindedness in everyday life

There are numerous everyday life occasions on which we can practise open-mindedness. First, when going into a situation where you might expect disagreement, ask yourself "how open or closed-minded am I now? What prejudices and preconceived opinions am I bringing to this situation?".

Then, when listening to someone with a different opinion, try very hard to see the situation from the other's viewpoint. Although they may be talking absolute rubbish as far as you are concerned, it probably makes a lot of sense to them. So try to understand why they hold that view, what it means to them.

You can also cross-examine yourself. When you disagree with someone, ask yourself, "Why?"; "How do you know that it will not work?"; "Are you not being influenced by your reaction to the person, not the opinion?".

The characteristics of closed-minded situations given earlier in this section can form the basis of such internal cross-examination. Remember, too, to be on the lookout for gullibility, or being too open-minded.

Another way to control negative, closed or even hostile feelings towards someone else involves a simple imaginative idea. Imagine that these negative thoughts actually leave you, fly to the other person, like arrows, and then hurt them.

Is that what you want? So, you think that the person is silly, or lazy, or for some reason you do not like them much. But does that mean you would actually go so far as wanting to hurt them? Probably not. Disliking or disagreeing is one thing, but hurting is another. Besides, you might find that the "negative thought arrows" actually act a bit like boomerangs, and come back to hurt you as well!

If you start imagining things in this sort of way, you are quite likely to be able to remain more open-minded towards other people.

4.9 Method 9: Working with your higher and lower selves

We have already looked at the idea of our higher and lower self - or angel and beast, as we also called them - in chapter 2. Since our higher and lower selves are - by their very nature - always with us, affecting what we do and the way that we do it, it can be a most useful part of self-development to get to grips with them.

In fact, there are many aspects of both in our inner selves. It is almost as though we are made up of a committee, or team, whose members do not always get on too well! This exercise is designed as a way of helping you to get in touch with some of those members.

That is, can we recognise and use our higher selves, and recognise and control our lower selves?

Exercise for getting in touch with higher and lower selves

Write down some of your basic characteristics - that is, your personality, your good and bad features, your habits, your attitudes. To start with, a list of about a dozen is sufficient.

Your list probably includes a mixture of positive and negative characteristics. Indeed, you should aim to have roughly an equal number of each.

Having drawn up your list, read over it several times. You are not trying to learn or memorise it, but just to get an overall impression of it.

Now, read over the list several times; try to become familiar with your good and bad features. What circumstances bring out the good ones? The bad ones?

You should now have an insight into important parts of your inner self. Think about them. How do you feel about them? What would you like to do about them?

Obviously, any positive aspects are to be welcomed. It may be that you were already aware of your positive features. On the other hand, quite often people are very surprised at an emerging positive higher self; all too often we are just too unaware of our better aspects.

So, rejoice and determine to capitalise on your positive qualities by calling on them and using them when appropriate! Look out for opportunities to use them at work and at home. And when you do use them, be aware of the fact.

What, though, of your negative aspects. Well, it is important not to be frightened of the faces of your "beast". Nor can you fight them - like many creatures from ancient myths and legends, they actually enjoy a fight, and get strength from the energy you put into fighting!

If you cannot fight the "beast", what can you do? Well, in fact you can tame it, or transform it. Every aspect of your lower self has its good features as well.

So start looking out for your beast, for your negative self in your everyday life. Try not to let it take charge without your noticing. Become aware of it, bring it into your conscious self. Then tame and transform it.

The task of transforming the beast involves trying to come to terms with it, and not allowing it to take control over you. Put your higher self in charge. When the bully tries to rule you - tell it to stop. When the lazy idler is in charge - tell it to get up and do something. At the same time, try to capitalise on its particular good features. Use the bully's strength in a positive way; use the coward's sense of danger to act as a protector of others; if your lazy idler has a sense of humour, use it to cheer up other people.

In summary, then, come to terms with your lower self; do not fight it, but move towards it, acknowledge it; recognise when it is trying to take charge, and control it; then transform it by converting its positive aspects and putting them to good use.

Helping other people work with their lower selves

All too often, when we see someone else's "beast" (that is, their lower self, or unattractive characteristics) in action, we only respond in a negative manner, by attacking, criticising, avoiding.

In fact, we cannot fight, or tame, another person's lower self. All we can do is to help them do so for themselves by giving them support and by making it clear that although we do not like what it is they do when that part of them is in charge, we none the less do still like them overall, as a whole person. This is the only way they will be able to gain sufficient inner strength to work on their own "beast".

The same is true for ourselves, of course. If others are constantly criticising, making negative remarks, attacking, then we will merely become defensive and insecure. In those circumstances, we are easy prey to our negative inner aspects!

So, although it is particularly hard to be tolerant with someone whose "beast" is on the rampage, that is when such an approach is particularly necessary. Otherwise we will just enter into another round of conflict and mutual anti-development.

4.10 Suggestions for further reading

Ferrucci, P. What we may be. Wellingborough, Turnstone Press, 1982.

Krystal, P. Cutting the ties that bind. Wellingborough, Turnstone Press, 1982.

Maltz, M. Psycho-cybernetics. New York, Prentice-Hall, 1960.

Rosenblatt, D. Your life is a mess: And what to do about it. New York, Harper and Row, 1976.

Simon, S.G. Meeting yourself halfway. New York, Argus, 1974.

SOME WAYS OF IMPROVING YOUR THINKING

5

In this chapter we will look at five ways of working on your thinking, memory, logic and creativity. The methods are

(10) reading;

(11) notetaking;

(12) repertory grid;

(13) ways of remembering things;

(14) thinking logically.

5.1 Method 10: Reading

Every manager has to read. Similarly, you would not be where you are today if you could not read. And by definition you would not be reading this book! However, most of us have considerable scope for improving our reading skills.

In this section we will outline an approach to systematic reading, including a method for you to gain insight into some of your own reading habits. After that an alternative method (meditative reading) is described, as well as reading with a speaking partner. Method 11 then gives some hints on notemaking.

Let us start, then, with systematic reading. In this approach there are four main steps, namely having a purpose, making a plan, implementing your plan and reviewing.

Step 1: Purpose for reading

This may sound strange; we do not normally think about our purpose for reading something.

In fact, there are a great many possible purposes for reading something. For example, your purposes for reading this book may include one or more of the following:

- to decide whether or not to buy it;

- to decide whether or not to borrow it;

- to gain theoretical knowledge about self-development, so that you can write an essay about it;

- to gain practical ideas about self-development, so that you can carry them out;

- for enjoyment.

Clearly, your reading strategy will be very different, according to your purpose. With some of them, a quick skimming through will be sufficient. With others, a comprehensive overview is required. With proofreading, you will need to read every single word. With some of them (e.g. "to look as though you are busy"), you do not actually need to read it at all!

So, when reading something, first of all think about your purpose.

Step 2: A plan for reading

Your plan, then, will depend on your purpose. Questions to ask yourself when making your plan include:

- shall I skim through it first? (often a good idea);

- shall I start at the beginning, or jump about from part to part? (this depends, of course, on your purpose; but you will find that often it is in fact better to jump about a little);

- shall I take notes?

- shall I underline sentences in the book itself?
  (this tends to spoil the book - do not do so unless
  it actually belongs to you!);

- when and where shall I read?

Step 3: Implementing your plan

This is when you actually do your reading. If you
want to take notes, you should find method 11 helpful.

Step 4: Review

After reading for some time, ask yourself some review
questions, as in table 4.

If you compare your review with your plan and your
purpose, you should start to get an idea of the sort of
reading habits that you might try to improve. For example:

- when and why do you read?

- what do you do when you disagree with the author?

- what do you do when you cannot understand something?

- what sort of notes do you take? Why? How useful are
  they?

- how long can you read without needing a rest? Does
  this depend on the nature and purpose of your reading?

- are there some circumstances in which you find
  reading particularly easy? Or difficult?

Meditative reading

So far we have looked at a very structured,
systematic approach to reading. Meditative reading, on
the other hand, is somewhat different. Here, you only
read a very small part of the chapter or article - not
more than two or three paragraphs at most, and possibly
only a sentence or two.

Table 4. Reading review

READING REVIEW QUESTIONS	SOME SAMPLE ANSWERS
1. How long did I read?	— Only for 5 minutes, because I was interrupted. — For an hour, then I needed to stretch my legs. — For 10 minutes, then I realised that I disagreed with the author so much that I could not go on.

2. Did I jump forward at all?	— No; I plodded on.
	— Yes. I skimmed through the whole piece to get a quick picture first.
	— Yes. I jumped because:
	  — I could not understand it
	  — I knew this already
	  — I was bored
	  — I did not think it had anything to do with what I wanted to find out.

3. Did I go back to reread at all?	— No; I just kept going on, even when I could not understand it. — I reread because I was confused. — When I got to one part I thought there was a link with something earlier, so I went back to that and reread it.

4. Did I pause at all?	— Yes. I paused because
	  — I could not understand
	  — I needed a short rest
	  —'I was daydreaming.
	— I wanted to think about what I had just read.
	— I was working out how it related to something else I know about.

5. What sort of notes did I take?	— None. — Main headings. — Definitions. — Diagrams.
6. Why did I take notes?	— I wanted to remember it. — I do not know; I suppose it is a habit. — I wanted to rewrite it in my own words, so as to understand it.

You then meditate on the piece that you have read. That is, from time to time over the next few days you reflect on it, think about it, talk it over with somebody else.

All the time you are asking yourself

- what do I think about this?

- how does it relate to other things I know; to other things I think about?

- how do I feel about it?

- what do I want to do with it, or because of it?

- what am I prepared to do?

- what am I not prepared to do?

Obviously, it takes a long time to read a whole book using this approach! Indeed, you probably will not read the whole book, but just a limited number of parts of it. But that does not necessarily matter - it is a great mistake to think that books are there to be read all the way through. Far better to select a limited number of passages that are relevant to you at any particular time, and concentrate on those. After all, you can always read more of it later.

Reading with a speaking partner

A rather unusual approach to reading is to do it with a partner.

Obviously, it can be helpful to discuss what you read with other people. However, this is done after you have read it. In this method, however, you discuss with your partner whilst reading.

What does this involve? Quite simply, the two of you (or three or four, perhaps, if you were doing it in a small group) agree on the passage to read. One of you then reads the first paragraph, after which you stop and discuss it.

The other person then reads the second paragraph, again stopping for discussion. And so on.

Sometimes, of course, the paragraphs might be so short, or so integrated with the next one, that you decide to read two or three at once. Use your discretion.

What should you read?

Our publication cannot provide a list of readings that would be of equal interest to all readers. After all, if your development needs are unique and if you establish your own self-development programme, you may prefer, too, to determine and decide what you would read.

Managers are busy people and cannot spend too much time on reading books, articles and other literature. The problem therefore is what to choose to make best use of your limited time.

You could be guided by your personal inclination to some extent: for example, you may like reading about experiences of successful managers, or about new developments in communications. Even writings on topics that at first glance look quite remote from your work field may be the source of good practical ideas!

Secondly, there are topics about which you should read, because they are important to your organisation and to you personally. Today you will hardly find a topic on which there is no abundant literature - your problem is therefore how to select the particular books, articles, etc., which you should read, or at least glance through.

It should be your principle to look regularly at a small number of the best professional and business periodicals dealing with management and with your particular trade. There are, then, book reviews, bibliographies and abstracting bulletins, which provide summaries of a large number of recent articles and books.

Advice on what to read and help in choosing the most useful books can be requested from a local management centre (e.g. if you attend a seminar there), from colleagues, business partners, or a training director (if your organisation has one).

It also pays to keep in touch with local, national and international events. Reading newspapers and current affairs journals can help with this. As well as certain international magazines, there are also some excellent publications that concentrate on particular parts of the world. And do not become trapped into just reading specialist material – do not forget to read about cultural matters as well. We can gain a lot of insight – as well as enjoyment – by reading novels, plays and poetry.

5.2 Method 11: Note taking

Although perhaps mainly related to reading, taking notes can also be helpful in other situations, including lectures, public meetings, committee meetings, watching educational television.

A key question is "why do I want to take notes?". At school and university, all too often the reason was because you would be expected to memorise various facts and repeat them in an exam.

By the time you are reading this book you will probably be more interested in understanding things, and applying them, than in memorising as such (if you are particularly interested in ways of remembering things, see method 13).

In this section we will describe three ways of making notes.

Copying things out verbatim

This means either copying from a book, word for word, or trying to write down, again word for word, what a lecturer or speaker is saying.

In fact, the latter is impossible, unless you have learned some form of shorthand.

In any case, it is pretty pointless. Copying out, or writing down, is time-consuming, boring, and only really helpful if it is essential for you to remember something exactly (again, see method 13). Otherwise this method, although often used, is not recommended.

Table 5. Extract from useful notes

Assertion: putting people in charge of themselves

                    — Who am I?   grounded in high
                    — How am I feeling?   self-esteem
                    — What do I want?   (finding your ego?)

      :   open up for others

      :   need to check with others

Non-assertion: passivity
(but choosing not to be assertive is itself an assertive choice)

Distorted
  assertion: aggression (transform do not fight!)

Helpful notes

What is needed is a means of making helpful notes, that have meaning for you, but that do not necessarily have to be perfectly understandable by other people.

Notes should summarise the main points of the lecture or written material. So it is important to capture these important points, by writing down main headings, followed by key words. There is no need for grammatical sentences. Similarly, since the notes are written for you, it is often useful to use abbreviations and "codes" that you understand.

Do not be inhibited by trying to make your notes look neat and tidy. Often it is more helpful to jot things down on different parts of the page, not necessarily in conventional paragraphs.

Table 5 shows an extract from some notes taken during a lecture on assertion which illustrate some of these points.

Figure 15. Spidergram version of notes on assertion

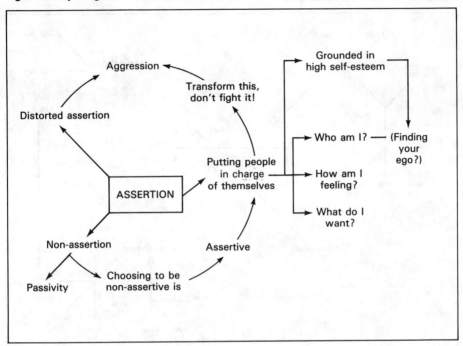

Spidergrams

    In figure 15 you will find a spidergram version of
the contents of table 5. This shows the contents of that
table in diagrammatic form, with lines linking up the
notes that relate to each other. As you can see, the
result is a network, with lines radiating out from the
centre and cross-lines joining various elements. Hence
the name "spidergram", since it vaguely resembles a
spider's web.

    Although a spidergram might appear a bit confusing at
first sight, it can provide a most useful way of making
notes and summarising ideas. It can show linkages - where
one idea connects with another - in a way that conven-
tionally written notes never can.

    Also, a spidergram only uses a minimum of words and
is in fact a much quicker way of making notes. This is
especially useful during lectures and talks. At the same
time this means that you can cover quite a wide area on
one sheet of paper.

101

Figure 16. Preparing a spidergram

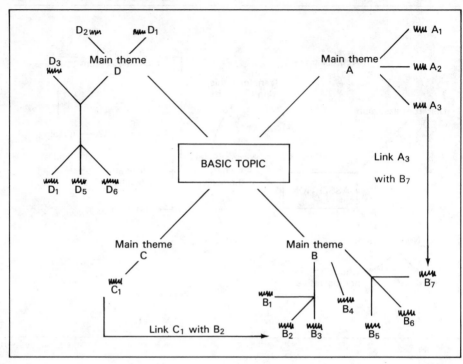

Another advantage is that the very method forces you to think. You have to choose the key words, ideas, concepts, phrases, to get at the real essence of what is being said or written.

When preparing a spidergram, you might find that you can simply go ahead and write it. You start with the basic topic being examined, and then mark off the main themes or subtopics as they occur, subdividing these as necessary. When cross-links occur, you can put these in (see figure 16).

You will almost certainly find that this is a bit of a messy business. Your diagram will have lots of lines crossing over, not enough space in one corner, and so on. However, once you have done it you can then redraw it more neatly.

If you find it too difficult to complete all in one go, as it were, then you can jot down very short notes on a sheet of paper, grouping them together in an approximate pattern. Then, when you have finished reading or listening, you can look for linkages and commonalities, before finally drawing the spidergram.

A third way is to prepare a number of small pieces of paper, and write each idea or note on a separate one. When you have finished, you lay all the pieces out, so as to get an overview. This can lead to a quick, first attempt at grouping particular points and ideas together. You can then go over them again, refining the groups, giving them names or descriptions, and showing the links between different groups (figure 17). Do not forget that these links can be negative as well as positive - that is, they can highlight contradictions, inconsistencies and opposing views and ideas.

Adding personal significance to your notes

Perhaps this is not so much a way of making notes as a means of using them.

It is very simple to describe, although it may not be so easy in practice! Basically, all it involves is reading over your notes carefully, and then noting down answers to those questions.

What have I read: or heard?	What do I think about these ideas? How do they relate to other things I know?
So what?	How do I feel about them? why?
Now what?	What do I want to do with them? as a result of them?

You will not develop from what you have read or heard unless you really engage yourself with it. Answering these questions will help with this process.

Figure 17. Preparing a spidergram in three steps

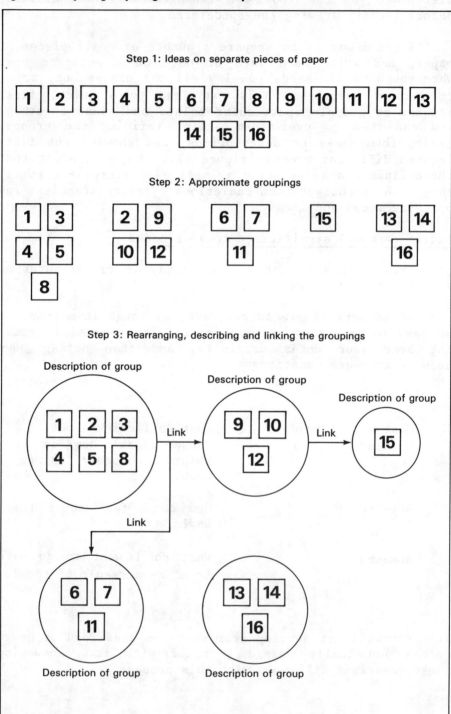

5.3   Method 12: Repertory grid

The term "repertory grid" is a slightly fancy name for an excellent technique of examining the way you think, feel or wish.

For example, it could be used to help you examine

- what it is about people that you get on well with compared with those you do not get on well with;

- what it is about those parts of your job that you do well compared with those parts that you do not do well;

- when do you find it relatively easy and difficult to exercise your will-power (see method 7);

- in what circumstances are you fairly open-minded, and closed-minded? (see method 8).

Once you have a clearer understanding of these issues, you should then be in a better position to do something about it - such as

- to get on better with certain people;

- to do certain parts of your job better or to try to delegate those to someone else;

- to work on improving your will-power;

- to work on being more open-minded.

We will describe the method step by step, illustrated by an example.

Step 1: Choose the theme or issue to examine

You will normally use the method to examine something that is troubling you, such as a problem, or a difficult decision.

For the example here, we will choose

"What is it about some people that makes me
get on well with them, compared with others
with whom I get on badly?"

Step 2: Identify some actual examples of the theme or issue

In this case, this means identifying some people who
you get on well with, and some with whom you do not. These
are listed below (about five of each is a good number).

I get on well with   I do not get on well with

    Mike   Roger
    Harry   David
    Jane   John
    Elisabeth   Sarah
    Malcolm   Richard

Similarly, you could list parts of your job you do
well and not well; actual situations when you could and
could not exercise your will-power; or whatever. It is
important that these be real examples, not hypothetical
ones.

Figure 18. Repertory grid (Step 3)

FEATURE	MIKE	HARRY	JANE	ELISABETH	MALCOLM	ROGER	DAVID	JOHN	SARAH	RICHARD
1.										
2.										
3.										
4.										
5.										
etc. — use a whole page										

106

Step 3: Draw up a repertory grid chart

Copy the chart shown in figure 18, and enter your examples.

Step 4: Write the examples on separate sheets of paper

Each example (in this case the 10 people) should be written on a small piece of paper. Thus, you will end up with ten pieces of paper, each with a name, situation, aspect of your job, or whatever on it.

Step 5: Make the first analysis

This involves shuffling the pieces of paper, and then taking any three of them at random. Then look at the examples written on these three, and decide which two are most like each other compared with the other.

For example, suppose I choose, at random, Mike, Malcolm, Sarah. Looking at these I see that Mike and Malcolm are similar to each other, compared with Sarah, because each of them is a man, she is a woman. That is:

Mike:

man   Sarah: woman

Malcolm:

I also notice that Mike and Malcolm are middle-aged, whilst Sarah is young.

Mike:

middle-aged   Sarah: young

Malcolm:

In other ways, though, I note that Mike and Sarah are similar (they are both my subordinates), compared with Malcolm (who is my boss).

Mike:

subordinates.   Malcolm: boss

Sarah:

107

Figure 19. Repertory grid (Step 5)

FEATURE	MIKE	HARRY	JANE	ELISABETH	MALCOLM	ROGER	DAVID	JOHN	SARAH	RICHARD
1. Man _____ Woman										
2. Middle-aged _____ Young										
3. Subordinates _____ Boss										
4. Friendly _____ Distant										
5. Get on well _____ Do not get on well										

Similarly, I find Mike and Sarah similar, in that they are friendly, whilst Malcolm is distant.

Mike: Malcolm: distant
       friendly
Sarah:

Again:

Mike: I get on   Sarah: I do not
          well with   get on well
Malcolm: with

As I note these characteristics, I enter them in the left-hand column of the table, as shown in figure 19.

Step 6: Make further analyses

When you have got as many characteristics or features as you can from the first three, put those pieces of paper back in the pile, shuffle, and take three more. It does not matter if one or two have already been chosen; indeed, if you carried the exercise to its logical conclusion you would do so until every possible combination had appeared - which would take a very long time.

Figure 20. Repertory grid (Step 7)

FEATURE		MIKE	HARRY	JANE	ELISABETH	MALCOLM	ROGER	DAVID	JOHN	SARAH	RICHARD
1.	Man ———— Woman	L	L	R	R	L	L	L	L	R	L
2.	Middle-aged ———— Young	L	R	L	R	L	R	R	R	R	R
3.	Subordinate ———— Boss	L	L	O	O	R	L	L	L	L	O
4.	Subordinate ———— Equal	L	L	L	R	O	L	L	L	L	R
5.	Boss ———— Equal	O	O	O	R	L	O	O	O	O	R
6.	Get on well ———— Do not get on well	L	R	L	L	L	R	R	R	R	L
7.	Friendly ———— Distant	L	L	L	R	R	R	L	R	L	R
8.	Makes me feel insecure ———— Makes me feel safe	R	L	R	R	R	L	L	R	L	L
9.	Seems to share my basic values ———— Disagrees with my basic values	L	R	L	L	R	R	R	L	R	R
10.	Good sense of humour ———— No sense of humour	L	L	L	R	L	R	L	R	L	L
11.	Seems to like me ———— Seems to dislike me	L	R	L	L	L	R	R	R	R	L

Using now this second set of three examples, do the same analysis, and again enter the features in the table. Some of them, of course, will start to reappear - do not put them in twice.

Continue this process with several sets of three, until you have between 15 and 20 features.

Step 7: Complete the table

You now have to score each of the examples according to the various features that you have elicited. Figure 20 shows our example.

You take each feature in turn, and put marks in each of the columns in that feature's row. In our example, taking feature No. 1 (man _____ woman), we put L (i.e. left hand) against every man, R (right hand) against every woman.

In the next row (middle-aged _____ young), it is L for every middle-aged one, R for each young one.

Then in row three (subordinate _____ boss), it is L for each subordinate, R for each boss. If someone is neither (e.g. an equal) they get an O.

Row 4 (subordinate _____ equal) gives L for subordinates, R for equals, O for bosses. And so on.

Step 8: Analysing the table

Analysing is the hardest part. You have to look for patterns, or correlations, between the rows (i.e. between the features).

Some stand out quite clearly; for example, rows 6 and 11 give an exact correlation (i.e. L in row 6 with L in row 11. R with R every time). This tells you that people you get on well with are those whom you see as liking you. And, of course, vice versa – you believe that those you get on well with like you (you may be wrong, of course).

You also look for cases of clear negative lack of correlation, or consistent disagreement. For example, rows 8 and 9 are in almost complete disagreement (i.e. L in row 8 goes with R in row 9, and vice versa). This tells you that people whose values differ from yours (row 9, R) make you feel insecure (row 8, L).

Other patterns also emerge. In this instance, you will find that you do not get on well with young subordinates, although you do get on well with middle-aged ones, also with young equals.

There is no particular pattern between rows 6 and 7; this tells you that whether or not you get on well with someone does not seem to depend on whether they are friendly or distant.

Similarly with rows 6 and 10 – so there is no connection between your getting on with someone and whether or not they have a sense of humour.

Finally, there is quite a close link between rows 7 and 10 – you associate friendliness with having a sense of humour.

Step 9: So what?

The final step is to decide what, if anything, this means to you.

So, ask yourself

- what do I think about this analysis?

- what do I feel about it?

- what do I want to do about it?

- what am I prepared to do? What am I not prepared to do?

In the worked example, you might decide that the analysis is fairly accurate. You feel surprised. You were not aware that it is young subordinates who you have the greatest difficulty with. You resolve to improve this position. Your first steps will include

- taking more care when dealing with young subordinates;

- asking them for feedback about how they see you.

Again, you are not happy to realise that people whose values differ from yours make you feel insecure. You resolve to try to be more open-minded about this. As a first step you will carry out the exercise on this subject (method 8).

Summary

Although all this may sound rather cumbersome, once you get the hang of it the repertory grid can provide a most useful way of becoming aware of how you see things; how you feel about them; what you think of them; how you respond to them.

At first, you might find the overall analysis (step 7) rather difficult. However, even if you only get as far as filling out the table (step 6), this in itself will tell you quite a lot about yourself. Although the repertory grid can clearly be done on your own, it also lends itself to working with someone else, or in a small group.

Your partner can quiz you about the features, helping you to see some that you had overlooked. The same is true in getting the overall analysis, and in deciding what to do about it (steps 7 and 8).

5.4 Method 13: Ways of remembering things

In this section, three ways of remembering things are described, namely using a notebook; systematic memorising technique; backwards review.

Using a notebook

Why bother to try to remember things when you do not really need to? In other words, there is a way of reminding yourself of things without having to rely on your memory.

Quite simply, it involves carrying a small notebook or notepad with you at all times. Whenever something important occurs to you, or you realise something you will have to do, or you are given some information, then write it down in the notebook.

Writing it down may well help you to remember it. But that is not the main purpose. What you can now do is refer to your notebook regularly, to see what you have to do, or tell somebody, or get for a friend, or whatever it is.

Systematic memorising technique

Although using a notebook can serve as a self-reminder, there may well be times when you really do want to memorise certain information.

There is a useful systematic process for helping you to memorise something:

(1) Concentrate on it; pay full attention. It is much easier to memorise something if you are not distracted by noises, other people, things that are happening.

(2) Recite it. Write it out several times, recite it to yourself or out loud. Go over it from memory as soon

as you can, correcting errors as soon as possible after you finish. This is easier to do in short bursts, so if you are trying to memorise a long definition or passage from a book, split it into a number of shorter parts first.

(3) Visualise it; make a picture. Try to imagine it in your mind's eye. If it is a set of instructions, imagine yourself carrying it out. If it is a definition, imagine the object, see it as it is described.

(4) Relate it to something else. Try to see if it reminds you of something - something that looks the same; feels the same; smells the same; or, conversely, something that is clearly quite different - use a contrast as a way of remembering it - for example, compare it with something that is much bigger, smaller, rougher, smoother, or whatever.

(5) Make up a memory aid, or mnemonic. This is a sentence that has words beginning with the initial letters of what you are trying to remember. For example, this systematic approach to memorising consists of Concentration, Recitation, Visualisation, Relating, Mnemonic. So, a mnemonic to remember those steps could be Can Root Vegetables Replace Meat?

Backwards review

The regular carrying out of a backwards review at the end of each day (method 2) will also help to develop your powers of memory.

5.5 Method 14: Improving your ability to think logically

Your powers of logical thinking - i.e. your ability to think about links between ideas, causes and effects - will be increased if in fact you practise using them.

Obviously, there are many everyday situations where you can try to do this. At the same time, there are a number of special exercises that will help as well.

One of these has already been described - backwards review (method 2). This helps you to follow a particular path of action, after the event, involving you in a process of examining cause and effect, in a way that should sharpen up your powers of logic.

Four other exercises are not described, which also require you to examine the way things and ideas are linked, with one leading to another. These are: logical trees or flow charts; contemplation on physical objects; contemplation on abstract ideas; a particular meditation.

Logical trees or flow charts

Strictly speaking, there are special rules for preparing flow charts and logical trees, but we will not be quite so particular here, and we will ignore some of the more technical aspects of their construction.

One use for flow charts is as an aid for systematic planning. Suppose, for example, you want to organise a public meeting. First write down the various things that need to be done. Do not bother yet about what order they go in, just collect together all the various steps. Your list might look like this

- send out announcements;

- book a room;

- ask a guest speaker;

- arrange for refreshments.

You then look over these, and note that some must be done before others. For example, you cannot send announcements until you have fixed the speaker. So you write these like this, figure 21 (step 1). Now, if you are thinking carefully, you will realise that something is missing. It is all very well to ask the speaker, but you really must make sure that he or she has accepted before sending out the announcement. So the diagram is redrawn as step 2. What if the speaker refuses? Well, step 3 shows this.

That is fine; you have probably got the idea by now. Figure 22 shows a more complete picture of this little plan. You will notice that a number of extra

Figure 21. Flow chart (Steps 1-3)

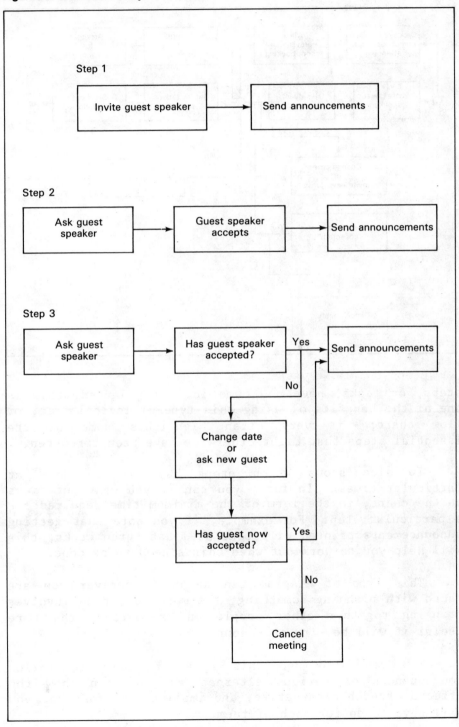

115

Figure 22. Completed flow chart

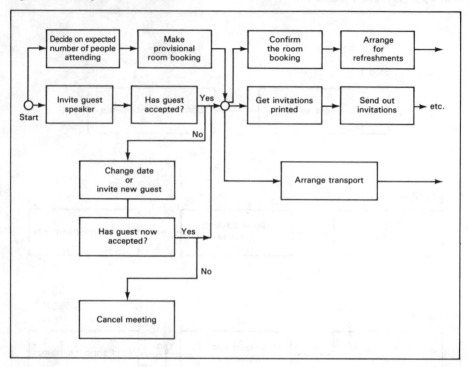

steps, or tasks, have now come into it. Indeed, this is one of the benefits of using this type of logical tree, or flow chart; it very often highlights some of the essential steps that might otherwise have been forgotten.

It also shows which steps have to be done at particular times. In fact, you can if you want put times on the chart, in the form of the minimum time required for a particular step. For example, if you note that getting announcements printed will take at least three weeks, this will help you to work out when things need to be done.

This type of diagram can be used whenever you are faced with planning something; the more your plan involves bringing together other people and resources, the more useful it will be. Try it - soon.

You can also use this type of chart to follow consequences of various alternatives. It can show the effects of each alternative, and implications for what you will have to do for each of them.

Once you get used to thinking in this way, it can become a most useful discipline for thinking logically about the implications and consequences of various plans and actions.

The same idea can be used to look at the way that ideas and theories link together. In fact, this has already been described in method 11, where the diagrams were referred to as spidergrams. Do not forget to look out for the ideas that may contradict each other (that is, they are illogical), as well as those that relate positively.

Contemplation on physical objects

This is an excellent way of getting your mind used to thinking about links, consequences, implications and other aspects of logical thinking.

Quite simply, you take some physical object, and then think about it and everything to do with it.

As an example, take this book. First, the paper. Think of the trees that were cut down, then made into pulp, then into paper. The paper went to the printer, who brought in ink, type, and people to print it. Then to the binder. And when it was bound, how did it get to you? How was it transported? By sea? Then think of the ship, the sailors, the docks, the customs men, the lorries, the roads. The links in the chain are endless (and you have not even thought of the author, and all the links and connections that went into writing the book in the first place!). Even the most simple object will have links with all sorts of people, and other things. By doing this exercise regularly, you will not only develop your powers of logical thinking, but you will also be combining thinking about small parts with getting an overview - another aspect of developed thinking.

Contemplation on abstract ideas

This is a bit similar to the last exercise, but is perhaps somewhat more difficult. Instead of thinking about something physical, you choose a personal quality as the object on which to meditate.

You can use any personal quality you like - although it is better to choose a positive one, at least to start with. Suitable qualities include

- courage	- cheerfulness	- calm
- faith	- kindness	- humour
- openness	- gratitude	- sacrifice
- hope	- freedom	- beauty
- love	- peace	- creativity
- wisdom	- understanding	- will-power
- truth	- unselfishness	- strength
- joy	- happiness	- understanding

How do you reflect on a quality? You think about it for 10 to 15 minutes, noticing what it means to you, when you experienced it in yourself, when you experienced it in others, what effect it has, where it comes from, and so on. Anything does, as long as it is about the quality in question. Keep going for at least 10 minutes. Do not give up when tempted, thinking that you have chosen the wrong one for you - they are all for you, and it is by keeping going that you will really start to develop insights and intuition, as well as sharpen up your powers of logical and analytical thinking.

A particular meditation

If you find contemplation on abstract ideas too difficult, this meditation may provide an excellent substitute.

In this case, you choose a word, an idea, an image, a quality, or an object, to think about. To start with, you should choose something nice or positive, like "flower", "kindness", "food", "this book".

You then get into a comfortable position, as for meditation, and think about your chosen word or whatever. Soon, another word or idea will come into your mind. Examine it for three or four seconds, then back to the original.

Figure 23. A particular meditation

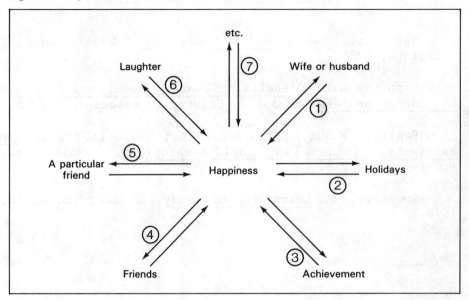

And so on. Figure 23 shows an example of what might happen, using "happiness" as the starting word. As you can see, sometimes the same word comes up more than once. That is fine.

It is important to return to the starting word each time; in this respect it is quite a different technique from the earlier two. If a cluster of connections does arise, go back to the centre between each link.

As well as helping to develop your ability to link things, ideas and people together, this should also give you a lot of insight into yourself and the way you see the world.

5.6 Suggestions for further reading

Adams, J.L. Conceptual blockbusting: A guide to better ideas. San Francisco, W.H. Freeman, 1974.

Bolles, R.N. What colour is your parachute? Berkeley, Ten-Speed Press, 1979.

de Bono, E. The five-day course in thinking. Harmondsworth, Penguin, 1971.

119

Buzan, T. Use your head. London, BBC Publications, 1974.

Ferrucci, P. What we may be. Wellingborough, Turnstone, 1982.

Lippitt, G.L. Visualizing change: Model building and the change process. La Jolla, University Associates, 1973.

Pedler, M.J.; Burgoyne, J.G.; Boydell, T.H. A manager's guide to self-development. Maidenhead, McGraw-Hill, 1978.

Rowntree, D. Learn how to study. London, Macdonald, 1970.

SOME OTHER OPPORTUNITIES
FOR SELF-DEVELOPMENT

6

In this chapter we will look at five classical and quite traditional ways of developing yourself as a manager - namely:

(15) courses, including correspondence courses;

(16) packages and programmed texts;

(17) special projects;

(18) joining associations and professional bodies;

(19) writing for journals;

(20) teaching and training others.

6.1 Method 15: Courses, including correspondence courses

Going on a course is perhaps one of the best known, most commonly recognised methods of self-development.

In fact, as this book shows, the course represents only one of a large number of approaches to conscious, systematic self-development. Going on a course may have several disadvantages over other methods, including:

- expense; both financially and in terms of time;

- inconvenience; you can only go on a course when the course is being run, and you have little or no say in that (whereas most of the other methods can be done when and where you want);

- irrelevance; few courses are designed around the specific needs and issues of participants. They tend to be subject or discipline-based, rather than being built around real life problems and self-development questions.

However, we are not trying to say that courses have no place in one's self-development. They certainly can be useful. To make them useful, though, it is a good idea to ask several questions.

Purpose

- why do I want to go on the course?

- what are my real motives?

    . to learn certain things? Why? How will these help me?

    . to obtain a qualification? Why?

    . for prestige, or will it really help me? How?

    . to get an opportunity to go overseas?

    . for a rest, or break from work?

- will going on this particular course achieve these aims? What makes me believe this?

- what alternatives are available?

Feasibility/convenience

- what are the entry requirements? Can I meet these?

- how much will it cost?

- do I have this money? Can I justify spending it in this way?

- are there any sources of funding? (e.g. my employer; government; training fund; external aid agency);

- how long will the course last? What will be the effect of my being away for that length of time?

- where will it be held? How will that affect me?

- who else will be affected if I go on a course? In what way will they be affected?

Quality of the course

- what evidence is there that the course will achieve its stated aims? (NB: courses are big business these days and as such are being strongly marketed. Many false and misleading claims are made about all sorts of courses, particularly, we are sorry to say, in the field of management training);

- do you know anyone else who has actually been on the particular course? What does he or she say about it? Is there a continuing relationship between your organisation and a particular institution or course?

- if it is a qualification course, try to obtain figures of the pass/fail rates. Reputable institutions should give you these if you ask. If the course is overseas (e.g. in the United Kingdom or the United States), try to find out how many "foreign" students attend the course, and how their pass/fail rates compare with those for local students. It is a sad fact that quite a number of institutions these days are making up numbers on their otherwise undersubscribed courses with overseas students, for whom the course is not really suitable, but who may be charged higher fees than local students;

- find out about facilities for overseas students, such as accommodation and arrangements for practical project work.

Correspondence course

The same points apply to selecting a correspondence course, although there is probably not so much money or time at risk. On the other hand, learning by correspondence is much more difficult than most people imagine.

One of the problems is that most correspondence courses do not give enough guidance on how to study and learn but concentrate solely on the subject matter.

Before taking up a correspondence course, ask for a sample lesson. Also, ask the correspondence college if there is anyone in your part of the world who has done the course, so that you can get in touch with him or her to get their opinion of it. Sometimes the lessons take the form of "model answers"; although these appear useful at first sight, they can become quite a hindrance. "Model answers" will probably enable you just about to pass an exam, but in no way will they help you become an outstanding student. Although harder work, it is better not to be given model answers to learn, but to have to work out your own essays and ideas, with proper feedback from correspondence tutors. So ask for a sample lesson, do a sample assignment, and get a sample feedback.

Many correspondence colleges offer a discount if you pay the whole fee in advance. Unless this is particularly attractive, it would be better to pay by instalments so that if you find it does not live up to its claims you will have minimised your financial loss.

In some countries there are a growing number of programmes which combine correspondence courses with radio or television programmes, local discussion groups, and so on. These may well offer a much better and more effective way of learning than a correspondence only approach, especially if this is being conducted from some form of institution thousands of miles away.

When doing a correspondence course, you have to decide when and where to do your studying. It is very important to try to study at regular times, with a definite timetable (e.g. two hours every night; or three hours on Tuesdays and Thursdays; or every Sunday morning). The amount of time you spend will naturally depend on the nature of the course; a good correspondence course will adivse you on this. In fact, many students think that such guidance is exaggerated (i.e. too many hours are recommended). However, very often in practice you will find you need to spend more than suggested, rather than less. Surveys have also shown that the majority of correspondence students spend far less time studying than they originally intended - so keep this in mind in preparing your plan.

Since taking on a correspondence course really is a major commitment, you are advised not to do so until you have really thought about your long-term plan for self-development (see chapter 2 and appendix 4 on "biography work").

As already stated, irrespective of the total amount of time it is very important to plan to work regularly - make yourself a timetable, and try to stick to it. Of course, unforeseen events will sometimes force you to deviate from it. When this happens, try not to panic, but catch up as quickly as possible.

Your timetable should include:

- how many hours a week you will study;

- how these hours should be spaced out;

- what times of day you are going to use, which depends on times available, and your personal preferences and circumstances; some people work best early in the morning, others late at night;

- how they will be divided amongst your subjects;

- how long any one period of study should be - in fact, between 45 minutes and two hours; you will need a break before working any longer.

Where you study will again partly be determined by your circumstances. However, in general, it is far better to work at a table or desk, rather than lying down or sitting in an armchair. Do not forget that much of the time you will be taking notes. Remember, too, that it is very difficult to concentrate if there is a radio or TV on, or children playing, or other distractions.

Correspondence study is a difficult and, often, a lonely process. Take heart! Nearly all correspondence students get depressed and feel like giving up - so you are not on your own!

When you encounter difficulties, try not to give up; rather, use the difficulties as opportunities for learning to learn. Careful analysis of your difficulties should enable you to gain considerable insight into your blocks to learning; this feedback can then be the starting point of a cycle of development, using the self-assessment and planning processes described in chapter 2.

If possible, choose a correspondence course with two-way communication (e.g. a counselling system, or telephone teach-ins). This may not be possible in many parts of the world - but why not try to establish such a system of your own? Try to find some fellow-students, and form a self-help group (method 27). Or ask your local college or management institution to set up a counselling service (see also chapter 10).

The main processes of correspondence study are reading, notetaking and writing essays. The first two of these are discussed elsewhere (methods 10 and 11).

Writing essays

Writing essays is a skill in itself. In brief, the following guidelines may be helpful:

- make sure you understand the essay topic; analyse the title and ask yourself some related questions, as though you were an examiner testing yourself on the topic;

- as you read and research an essay, keep this question in mind, and ask others as you go along; write all the questions down, as a reminder;

- keep a little notebook with you, and jot down any ideas relevant to particular essay(s) as they occur to you. This will often be at unexpected moments, and keeping a notebook like this is a guard against forgetting these often creative and brilliant ideas!

- when you see something written, make a note of the author, the title, publisher, date, page number;

- plan the essay, either in a logical flow, or using a spidergram (method 11);

- use a structure such as

    . introduction;
    . main body;
    . conclusion;

- write in an appropriate style, using everyday
  language if possible;

- when it is written, put it aside for a few days, then
  re-read it and amend it if you want to. You may have
  to discipline yourself to rewrite it to improve it.

6.2 Method 16: Packages and programmed texts

An increasing number of "packages" for self-
development are gradually becoming available. What do we
mean by "package"? They usually come in the form of a
book (sometimes a loose-leaf manual), consisting of a
number of suggested exercises and activities, that are
designed to help with various aspects of self-
development. In that sense, this book can be seen as a
package.

Programmed learning books and packages differ from
this one in that they are usually more concerned with
theoretical, subject matter rather than with personal
skills. They present this matter in a particularly
structured, logical manner, which requires the user to
make some form of active response (usually by answering a
question) before moving on to the next bit.

There is a rapidly growing number of audio-visual,
video, and computer-based programmes and training
packages. These can incorporate quite clever features,
and can have a lot to offer for self-development, although
it is important to think about the relatively high cost,
reliance on imported equipment (that is likely to go wrong
without expensive maintenance facilities, and that itself
depends on electricity supplies that are often erratic),
and dependence on equally costly imported programmes.
None the less, this is probably an important area for the
future.

6.3 Method 17: Special projects

Another way to widen your range of experiences – and hence to increase your opportunities for self-development – is to undertake special projects at work.

Of course, you may feel that you are busy enough already, without taking on anything extra. However, it is certainly worth looking into the possibility of carrying out a special project.

What might this involve? Well, it all depends. Talking with your boss or other colleagues should high-light all sorts of areas or problems that need investigating. Try to choose something that is of real relevance to your organisation – look for areas where things are going wrong; or cost too much; or where important changes are about to take place. If there is a management services specialist in your organisation, he or she might well be able to give you guidance here.

If you are working with a self-development or action-learning group (see chapter 8), then doing a group project can be particularly rewarding.

There is also an increasing use of project work on courses; again, this may be done individually or in a group. Some of the phases that a group goes through are described in chapter 11. They are presented there for use by management trainers, but if you are a member of a trainer-less project group, much of what is said there will be of relevance to you.

6.4 Method 18: Joining associations and professional bodies

An excellent way of encouraging your self-development is to join some form of association, professional body, or whatever seems appropriate.

At the very minimum, this will put you in touch with other people who have similar interests to your own. Most such associations also produce regular journals and newsletters which can be a source of contacts, ideas and information (about people, courses, new publications).

You can also become a more active member, taking part in meetings and conferences, writing for publications, organising visits, and so on.

You may well know which associations exist in your locality. If not, you should be able to find out by talking with colleagues, looking in newspapers, enquiring at relevant institutions.

If there really is not a relevant association already in existence, then why not try to form one yourself? Call a meeting of people who might be interested, see if, between you, you can get it off the ground. That very process will be very good for your self-development.

6.5 Method 19: Writing for journals

As well as reading various journals and magazines, why not try writing for them? Most are extremely pleased to receive contributions - particularly from managers in organisations. Many journals seem to attract articles only from academics. Whilst some are happy with this, a large number would also be very pleased to publish contributions from real, practising managers.

If you want your article to have a reasonable chance of being accepted, it is important to bear in mind the style that seems acceptable to the journal in question. By reading several issues, you will get an idea of the sort of material they are looking for, the preferred length, whether it should be theoretical, practical, or both, and so on. Every journal has its own "personality", and you will have to bear this in mind.

If your article is rejected, do not be too disheartened. The fact that you made the effort is in itself an achievement - and anyway, you will probably have learned a lot in the process of writing it.

6.6 Method 20: Training and teaching others

An excellent way to develop yourself is by training and teaching others. As an effective manager you will be doing this as part of your job, on an everyday ad hoc basis. But why not consider offering your services to give sessions on training courses as such, either within your organisation or at a local college or institution?

Alternatively, you may have some skill or interest not directly associated with work (e.g. sport or a hobby). Again, a local college, youth club, or other community venture might well be only too pleased to have you work with them.

This work might involve direct coaching or instruction, or you might bring your managerial expertise to help run a club, committee, voluntary body, or whatever. So you will need to decide whether you want to train by giving direct instruction, or by working with others who can learn from your example.

6.7 Suggestions for further reading

James, D.E. A student's guide to efficient study. London, Pergamon, 1967.

Leedy, P.D. Read with speed and precision. New York, McGraw-Hill, 1963.

Morgan, C.T.; Deese, J. How to study. New York, McGraw-Hill, 1957.

Rowntree, D. Learn how to study. London, Macdonald, 1970.

Woodley, C.H. How to study. Sydney, Angus and Robertson, 1959.

Details of some relevant packages are given in the further reading at the end of chapter 3.

PHYSICAL FITNESS, RELAXATION AND OTHER ASPECTS OF THE SELF

7

In this chapter we will examine physical fitness, relaxation, and four other aspects of the self, thus:

(21) working with physical fitness, relaxation and meditation;

(22) working with your size, shape and appearance;

(23) working with people who are different;

(24) working with your temperaments;

(25) working with your managerial style.

7.1 Method 21: Working with physical fitness, relaxation and meditation

When human beings first evolved, they were constantly faced with threats from dangerous animals, warring bands, and so on. Their reaction to those threats was to get rid of them - either directly by fighting them, or indirectly by fleeing from them. To help with that fight and/or flight, the human body prepared itself in various ways, including increased rate of breathing, raised blood pressure, faster heart beats, and so on.

Whilst today's managers are seldom faced with danger from wild beasts, they certainly find themselves in a number of stressful situations, being involved in conflicts and negotiations, meeting difficult deadlines, making critical decisions, or dealing with dissatisfied customers, bosses and politicians.

Although these situations are very different from those faced by our ancestors, our body responds in exactly the same way - increased heart rate, blood pressure, etc. Unfortunately, these responses - excellent though they might be for preparing us to fight a wild beast or to run as fast as possible - do not help us to cope with managerial problems.

Worse still, since we cannot fight or run in our offices, the physical fight/flight body changes cannot be worked off.

The result can be seen in many ways. In the short term, our readiness to fight comes out in snapping or shouting, usually at someone who does not have the power to retaliate, such as a subordinate. How often do you have a go at some innocent person, because you are really passing on the ticking off that your boss gave you?

Our flight behaviour can be seen in numerous ways, including daydreaming, going to see someone "on urgent business", doing something else rather than facing up to the task in hand, even going to the toilet at a critical moment! Headaches and mysterious, elusive aches and pains also provide a socially acceptable escape route for being off colour, going home early or staying away from work.

In the long run, the body's unrelieved fight/flight responses can build up and lead to serious health problems.

All too often, people respond to symptoms of stress by taking tranquilisers, or smoking, or drinking alcohol. But all of these have very damaging effects on our health.

So it is preferable to look for other ways of managing tension and stress. In general, two broad approaches to this can be adopted - physical and mental.

In the East, the close connection between mind and body has long been recognised, whereas in the West this has only been appreciated more recently.

Because of this connection, the apparently "physical" activities are described together with the apparently "mental" ones. Although the link is not absolute, very often a programme of exercises designed to develop physical fitness will lead to mental, as well as physical,

Table 6. Western and eastern physical exercises

Western physical exercises	Eastern physical exercises
Running; walking; jogging cycling; weightlifting	Judo; karate; kung fu; hatha yoga; t'ai chi; k'ai men
"Physical jerks" - special exercises for particular muscles	
Swimming	
Competitive sports, e.g. tennis, squash, bowling	Various other yogas (which include more meditation)
Competitive team games e.g. football, cricket	
Also the Alexander technique is a form of "yoga" (eastern) developed in the West	

relaxation. Conversely, what looks like a "mental" technique (such as various types of meditation), will also develop various aspects of physical fitness.

There is also a big difference between the general approaches adopted in the East and West, particularly for physical fitness (table 6). The western methods tend to emphasise intense, vigorous, often competitive, exercise, leading to strengthened muscles and the ability to exert yourself. Eastern methods, on the other hand, tend to be much more smooth and flowing, leading to balance and a different, less abrupt, more economical type of strength. Indeed, perhaps in these exercises speed, agility and flexibility are more important than strength itself. Because of the greater link between mind and body, the eastern physical methods are more likely to lead to relaxation as well (indeed, the western emphasis on competitive sport, and a related obsession with "level" of fitness, often makes people extremely anxious and tense).

Methods for physical fitness

It is not possible, in a book of this length, to go into any sort of detailed description of methods for physical fitness. All we can do is to mention some, as in table 6.

A most excellent book, that gives detailed descriptions of all of these and many more, is called The complete book of exercises (see references in section 7.6). It includes guidance on how to choose appropriate exercises. For example, your body shape affects the type of sport that you will find easy to take up. As a rule people who tend to be thin, wiry and angular, will find it more easy to take up running, jogging, walking, cycling or bowling. Round, large and fattish individuals may prefer swimming, cycling, bowling, or archery, while muscular people do any of these sports easily. At the same time, certain activities lead to different types of benefit; some examples are shown in table 7.

Physical methods for relaxation: physical meditation

To some extent, all the physical fitness methods will lead to relaxation (with the possible exception of over-competitive sport). However, there are some physical techniques that are particularly useful for helping you to relax.

As you will see from table 7, the eastern methods (hatha yoga, t'ai chi and k'ai men) are in this category. Unfortunately, it is not feasible to describe these in this book, as to do so requires considerable space. This is partly because a large number of pictures and diagrams is necessary, and partly because they are far more than techniques - they are really ways of life, sort of "physical philosophies".

Indeed, this means that in fact they are hard to learn from a book - you really need a teacher. It is possible that there might be one somewhere near where you live, but clearly this will not be so for most people. The book already mentioned The complete book of exercises does show reasonably clearly some of the basics of each of these approaches.

134

Table 7. Benefits produced by various types of exercise

Activity	Good for
Jogging	Weight control; sleep; digestion; heart and lungs; leg muscles.
Swimming	Sleep; digestion; heart and lungs; all muscles.
Cycling	Weight control; sleep; digestion; heart and lungs; all muscles.
Archery	Balance; chest and arm muscles.
Bowling	Arm muscles
Judo; karate; kung fu	Balance; agility; heart and lungs; all muscles.
Hatha yoga t'ai chi k'ai men	Balance, flexibility, suppleness, posture, heart, inner organs, breathing, self-awareness, inner calm, relaxation.
Alexander technique	Moving towards physical meditation.

However, it is possible to give guidance, here, on a few other physical ways of relaxing.

Alexander technique

To be fair, the Alexander technique is also a "physical philosophy". However, three of its main activities can be described, and practised, quite simply.

The first is lying down with your head/neck on a pile of books. This is in fact an excellent way of relaxing. It is based on the fact that when we are tense, most of this tension passes through the back of the neck, on its way between the brain and the other parts of the body. So resting with your neck in the "Alexander position" helps to remove the tensions.

135

Using this method, you lie on your back, with your neck (at the point in line with your ears) resting on a small pile of books - paperbacks are best. You will need to adjust the height of the pile until you are comfortable - about six inches on average. You then draw up your knees, and place your hands on your chest. This can be relaxing in itself, but it is also an excellent position for other types of meditation (see later in this section).

The second basic Alexander activity is to do with the way you stand. As a special exercise, you stand, arms by your side, with your feet about six inches (15 centimetres) apart, parallel to each other. You then bend your knees slightly, at the same time pushing your bottom out backwards a bit. Tilt your head down a little, and then look straight in front of you by raising your eyes a little (but keeping your head slightly tilted down). Finally, whilst maintaining this posture, you imagine a force running up your body, from the floor to the top of your head and out to the ceiling. Hold this position (knees slightly bent, bottom out, head tilted, eyes up, imaginary force flowing up through your body) for two or three minutes, or longer, as you get used to it. Keep breathing regularly - do not hold your breath.

Once you have got used to this method, you can then practise it at any time you are standing.

The third Alexander activity is to do with sitting. Most of us sit in a bad posture, leaning backwards so much that we are really "sitting" on the middle of our backs.

The exercise, then, involves sitting on a hard stool or chair, with your feet flat on the ground (no shoes). When you have sat down, put your hands under your bottom and feel around for two quite distinct "bumps". These are your sitting bones - that is, the "bearings" that you should really be sitting on.

When you have located your sitting bones, remove your hands, place them on your knees, and if necessary, adjust yourself so that your weight is now resting on your sitting bones. Tilt your head down slightly, with eyes up, as with the standing exercise.

Then, again like the standing exercise, you imagine a

force moving up through your body, from your sitting bones, up to the top of your head and out. Maintain this posture for several minutes. Keep breathing regularly - do not hold your breath.

Again, once you are used to this technique, you can use it whenever you are sitting down - although soft chairs make it very difficult. If you want to do it for quite a long time you might find it easier to place a cushion between you and the chair back.

Breathing exercises can be very relaxing. Find a quiet place where you can sit down comfortably. It is important to be fairly straight and upright. Although some people like to sit cross-legged on the floor, this is not essential and you may be more comfortable in a chair. In this case sit with both feet on the ground, back straight, head up. Do not be too comfortable - you must not fall asleep. Alternatively you can use the Alexander lying down position as described above.

When you are comfortable, close your eyes and then consciously relax all your muscles, starting at the top of your head and moving down through your body to the tips of your toes. If you have difficulty in doing this, tell yourself that you are becoming more and more relaxed, that you are going deeper ... and deeper ... and deeper. It is often helpful to imagine yourself going down, in a lift; on an escalator; in warm water; to the bottom of the sea.

Breathe in through your nose, out through your mouth, saying a drawn out "aaa.....ah", and listen to your own breathing. As you become more relaxed you will notice your breathing becomes slower, deeper, and more restful. Notice that at the bottom of each breath (i.e. after breathing out) there is a pause before you begin to breathe in again.

When you have noticed these pauses, start counting backwards from ten to one. Count thus: breathe out: TEN: breathe in: breathe out: NINE: breathe in: breathe out: EIGHT: etc. Count in this way from ten down to one, then back up from one to ten, down from ten to one, and so on.

Stray thoughts may come into your head while you are breathing/counting. Do not worry about this; just let the thought come, do not dwell on it, let it go. Then go back to TEN and start counting again. Do not worry if you never reach ONE, especially in the early days.

Continue breathing/counting in this way for 15 to 20 minutes (although ten minutes may be easier to start with) at least once a day; twice is better. Keep a watch or clock handy, and check if you wish (otherwise keep your eyes closed). When you finish, remain sitting quietly for a few minutes, then stand up slowly.

Mental methods for relaxation: meditation

Although the main purpose of meditation is to help to relax - and thereby improve various aspects of physical health as well - other benefits also gradually arise. Indeed, the claimed effects of meditation are so wide-ranging that they appear almost too good to be true! Nevertheless, some of the benefits for which there is at least some supporting evidence include:

- inner calm;

- reduced anxiety;

- less stress and tension;

- lower heart beat;

- reduced blood pressure;

- greater resistance to disease;

- better sleep;

- improved mental health;

- better memory;

- increased powers of logical thinking;

- greater creativity;

- increased confidence;

- greater will-power;

- intuition;

- improved ability to relate to other people.

There are many, many, different techniques and exercises for meditation, so all we can do here is to give a small selection. Those described in this section are fairly "general" ones, with the main aim of reducing anxiety and tension; some of the other effects listed above will also probably arise. Meditations designed specifically to improve your powers of thinking and logic are given in method 14.

To be effective, it is absolutely essential to meditate regularly, over a period of time. Once a day, for 15 to 20 minutes, is a minimum. Any less, and no real results are likely.

Different meditational traditions recommend different postures for meditation. However, there is not any absolutely "best" or "correct" way of sitting. The main thing is to be comfortable, and it does not matter if you sit on the floor or on a chair. If you can sit fairly straight, so much the better. It is preferable to sit rather than to lie down, for these types of meditation.

Many meditations involve you in contemplating certain physical objects. An example is meditation on a seed.

The seed you choose should be from a plant that you know about. That is, you should have seen the plant in its various stages of growth and development, from first shoot to growth of leaves, to buds, to flowers, to seeds, to decay or regeneration, depending on the type of plant.

To meditate on the chosen seed, you place it in front of you, and notice its shape, colour, and any other visible features. Then you gradually think about the fact that if it is planted in the right kind of soil, a plant would slowly develop from it. Imagine to yourself the life forces in the seed which, although asleep at the moment, are waiting to be released. Then imagine the plant growing, slowly but surely. See it, in your imagination, emerging from the seed, pushing a shoot upwards towards the light, and roots downwards. Imagine those roots collecting water and minerals from the soil.

Imagine the shoot breaking into fresh air, opening out, receiving warmth and air, developing leaves. See the buds forming, then gradually opening out into flowers. Imagine the flowers in their various shapes and colours, the insects flying around them. See the new seeds developing, in whatever way they do for that plant, as the flowers die down. Then see, in your imagination, the way the seeds are carried to the ground, and what happens to the plant after that.

As well as seeing all this in your imagination, try to feel what it is like to be the plant at each stage. How does it feel to burst out of the seed? To push out of the soil into the sunlight? And so on.

Another type is the bubble meditation. Imagine that you are sitting on the bottom of a lake, or slow-moving river. The water is clean and clear. Every time a thought comes into your mind, "trap" it in a bubble of air, and let it rise slowly to the surface of the water. Watch it rise, allow it a few seconds before it bursts.

Do not do anything else with your thoughts - do not comment on them, chase them or follow them in any way. Just notice them, watch them rise slowly. If the same thought comes several times, do not be put off. Just put it in a bubble each time, and let it rise.

If you prefer, the thoughts can go into balloons that rise slowly into the sky. Or anything else that moves up, or past, slowly before disappearing.

You can also try meditation on silence. Imagine that you are walking up a hill or mountain. There may be streams, trees, birds, flowers, butterflies - whatever comes into your mind. However, as you get higher up the hill, the air gradually becomes quiet and still. All noises die away.

At the top of the hill, there is a temple, shrine, or holy place dedicated to silence. This temple can take any form and shape that you like.

You go inside the temple. It is totally silent. No sound has ever been heard in there. As you move further into the silent temple, you notice a shimmering ball of light, warm, but not hot; bright, yet soft and gentle.

140

You walk into this ball of silent light, and feel yourself engulfed in it, completely surrounded. It is all around you, and flows everywhere through your body. Remain in this ball of silent light for two or three minutes. Hear the silence; feel the light.

Then gradually come out of the ball of light, towards the temple's entrance, and go back outside onto the hilltop. Feel the breeze, hear the sound of birds as you slowly walk back down the hill.

An alternative is meditation on a colour. Imagine a white screen in front of your eyes, and then see, in your imagination, a coloured patch appear on that screen. You can either choose a colour before you start, or just wait until a colour appears.

You will probably find this quite difficult, and it may take several days before you can really see the colour in your imagination. Once you have managed to do this, you can then start to see the coloured patch in a specific shape - say a triangle. Later, add a circle. Then mix colours and shapes - red circle, yellow square. Try more complicated shapes.

Hobbies, cultural pursuits and similar

Another aspect of relaxation is developing a balance between material and spiritual, scientific and artistic, work and play, concentration and relaxation.

An excellent route into this balance is through creative hobbies and cultural pursuits, such as art, music, drama. You can enjoy these as spectator or listener or, better still, by taking an active part in them yourself. Never mind if you are not brilliantly skilful, why not have a go at playing an instrument, making models, painting, doing batiks, acting, singing, making pottery, photography, or whatever takes your fancy. Most of us have a repressed urge to be creative, just longing to be released into activity!

If you do not know where to start, look through hobbies or crafts section of your local library, or see what your friends do and what societies and clubs there are in your vicinity.

7.2 Method 22: Working with your size, shape, and appearance

There are some aspects of your physique that you cannot really change. Your height, for example, or your general shape (e.g. long and thin; muscular; bony; round). Or your facial features.

You might well ask "so what? Who wants to change these anyway"? That is a very fair question. However, it is surprising how may people would like to have a different physical appearance if they could. They really seem to be ashamed of their body, to hate it, or specific parts of it. However, since your body is part of you, hating bits of it is of course the same as hating bits of yourself. An unhealthy thing to do!

A useful exercise, then, is to try to come to terms with your body, accepting it for what it is. You can do this by first of all having a good look at yourself all over - using a mirror if possible. Take a really good look.

Then ask yourself "is any part of my body telling me something"? You can do this as a form of meditation (method 21). Get into a comfortable position, close your eyes and try listening to your body. This may sound strange, but the odds are that you will probably get some sort of "message" quite quickly. It helps to capture the message by saying it out loud to yourself.

Sometimes the message will be "please stop hating me". For example, your nose might say "please stop hating me for being so big, and start to like me because of the valuable work I do for you".

Yes, perhaps this does sound a bit weird! But it is only another aspect of getting in touch with your subconscious (method 4), and it really can work. So give it a try!

The effect of your appearance on other people

All too often we are unaware of the effect our appearance is having on other people. For example, if you are very large, how do you think this makes smaller people feel and behave?

142

The best way to find out this sort of thing is by asking. In fact, people are often very reluctant to give you feedback about your appearance, so you will need to help them to be honest and open to you. Alternatively, try to observe the way people react to your size or shape. Or try to imagine how you would feel and respond if you were in their position.

Perhaps you will then be able to modify your behaviour a bit, to make things easier for others. For example, if you are very tall, you might sit down when talking with shorter people, so as not to overpower them. Or you might stand a bit further away. The main thing is to try to be sensitive to others and the effect you are having on them.

As well as your body itself, your clothes can have a big effect on people, so try to find out about that as well.

7.3 Method 23: Working with people who are different

We all tend to see the world through our own eyes, as though we are "normal", and others are "different". For example, if you are a man, you will have a man's view of the world; it will be very difficult for you to imagine how a woman sees things.

The same is true for other types of "different" people. In table 8, write down in the right hand column what you are in (e.g. in my case man, English, middle-aged, Christian, middle class, employed, healthy, married).

Table 8. Various characteristics of a person

Sex Ethnic group Age group Religion Social class Employment status Health Marital status

Then try to think about how these characteristics affect the way you see the world, the way you behave. What particular sets of values come with these? What advantages? What disadvantages?

What other groupings are there in your organisation (that is, apart from women and men, what other ethnic groups, ages, religions, etc.)? What do you know about their view of the world? For a range of different groups, could you consider and complete the following statements:

(a) the advantages of being _____ are _____;

(b) the disadvantages of being _____ are _____;

(c) as a _____, my main concerns are _____;

(d) the values I share with other _____ are _____;

(e) the things I like and dislike about _____ are _____;

(f) I would not like to be _____ because _____.

Good managers - and indeed developed persons - are tolerant of differences, whilst being aware of the extent to which they are affected by the norms of their own grouping.

7.4 Method 24: Working with your temperaments

This section is based on one particular theory about the way we respond to things - that is, how we respond or react to people, to situations, and to things that happen. There are, of course, other models of temperament; we have chosen one particular one that we often use in self-development work.

According to this theory, there are four main response styles, known as temperaments:

- the melancholic;

- the stable;

- the lively;

- the changeable.

144

In fact, everybody has some of each of these four temperaments within them. However, one temperament is usually stronger, more prominent, than the other three.

If you have a strong melancholic aspect, you will tend to be moody, falling into fits of depression, feeling sorry for yourself, being pessimistic.

The stable temperament shows itself in a desire for a quiet life, for predictable routine. Although you may have strong feelings about things, you will remain cool and calm in most situations.

If your temperament has a strong lively element, then you will be "fiery", full of energy, excited, likely to be talking a lot, expressing your own views, having quarrels or fights with people who disagree. A short temper, very quick to react.

Finally, the changeable temperament comes over as being interested in all sorts of things, without ever spending enough time at any one to become a specialist. "Jack of all trades, master of none", is a phrase used in English, to describe someone who flits about from one thing to another, never settling down or taking anything seriously, a bit like a butterfly. These people have lots of acquaintances, but few real long-term friends.

Temperament and self-development

As with many other aspects of self-development, the task here is to become aware of your temperament, and the effect it is having on you. By bringing it into your consciousness, you are then more likely to be in control, to realise what is happening, to take charge of yourself.

For example, suppose you suffer a disappointment. If you have a large melancholic component, you will feel this setback for days. You will become depressed, un-motivated, listless. You will suffer - and make others suffer around you! However, if you are aware of this, you are much more likely to be conscious of what is happening, and say to yourself "come on, pull yourself together. It is not the end of the world. Do not let my melancholic part dominate me".

Or, take another example. Suppose you are trying to

145

study something - or work with one of the exercises in this book. If you have a strong changeable part of you, you will not be able to settle down to concentrate. After five minutes you will be jumping up to do something else, or will be rushing out to visit a friend. But again, if you can be aware of this, you are on the road to saying "come on, changeable, settle down and get on with the task in hand".

Both these examples were negative. Of course, though, each temperament also has its positive aspects. Table 9 shows some of the good and bad features of each temperament. For example, in the case of a disappointment, you would be helped by bringing in either a stable or a changeable element - the first would say, "Never mind, do not get upset, keep going", the second would say, "Who cares, I will turn my attention to something else".

Working with temperaments in everyday life

One of the best ways to work with your temperament is, then, to be aware of it. When something happens, try to see which temperament is coming through in the way you respond, and, if this is not helping the situation, try to control it.

If you keep an incident diary of some sort (method 3), you might keep a lookout to see if there is any pattern in the way your temperament emerges. Does it change according to time of day? Or type of situation? Or person you are with? You could be quite sophisticated and do a repertory grid (method 12), dividing the "examples" along the top row of figure 18 into four groups, i.e. situations in which each of the four temperaments dominated, then seeing what other characteristics come in down the "features" column.

7.5 Method 25: Working with your managerial style

Just as with theories about temperaments, there are different ways of looking at managerial style. A common one uses a spectrum of behaviour, from autocratic to consultative, then participative, then laissez-faire. However, for consistency, here we will use one that is based on the same archetypes as used in chapter 1 for the skills of self-development, and in chapter 8, working with a speaking partner.

146

Table 9. Temperaments

Temperament	Feelings	Negative effects of feelings	Potential positive effects of feelings
Melancholic	Deeply felt inner experience	Moody, depressed, suffering, pessimistic, grumbling and complaining	Sympathetic, understanding how other people feel, compassion, good listener
Stable	Feelings don't often affect response, which remains calm most of the time	Lazy, withdrawn, fatalistic, uncreative, dull	Quiet, thoughtful, thorough, faithful, painstaking, dedicated, excellent at administration and organising things
Lively	Strong, quick outward reactions	Domineering, always wants to be in charge, full of sense of own importance, liable to lose temper, intolerant	Source of strength and inspiration, good leader
Changeable	All over the place	Superficial, unstable, never settling down to anything, always on the move	Source of many ideas, creative, humorous, charming

You will notice that in the table there is a column describing how a style can get distorted. All too often we fall into the trap of these distortions, imagining that we are being highly effective! For example, when we should be firm and strong, we become aggressive and bullying. Or in our desire to be fair and open-minded, we become weak-willed and gullible.

There is no "best" managerial style. Or, put another way, the "best" one is the one that is most appropriate at a particular time. You have to judge which is needed, taking into account the situation and the other people involved.

A good manager therefore needs to be able to recognise which style is needed at a particular time, and to be able to behave in that style.

In fact, most of us have a predominant style - one that comes through more readily than others. Looking through table 10, can you see which style you seem best at? Which comes most readily to you? Which type of situational need are you most easily able to help with?

147

Table 10. Managerial styles

STYLE	THIS STYLE IS NEEDED AND USEFUL WHEN...	BUT BEWARE OF DISTORTING THE STYLE BY...
Confronting	• you need to assert yourself, to stick up for your ideas • you disagree with somebody, and need to tell them so • you want to point out inconsistencies in what someone is saying • you want to challenge somebody's assumptions • an initiative is needed, e.g. proposals for action	• becoming aggressive, bullying, intolerant, overbearing, domineering
Supporting	• someone needs help and support • someone is talking, and hoping that you will listen • you want to be tolerant, open-minded and patient • someone is trying to speak but cannot get a word in edgeways, or is having difficulty expressing themselves	• being too soft-hearted • becoming apathetic, withdrawing • being gullible, allowing yourself to be influenced by another person
Theoretical	• relevant theories can be used to explain a situation or to help in solving a problem • you are trying to make generalisations from something that has happened • you are trying to pass an exam	• becoming too carried away by theories, thus losing touch with real problems and with common sense • using theory as an end in itself • rushing to textbooks and experts for the solution to every problem • falling into the trap of thinking that book knowledge and wisdom are the same
Practical	• something needs to be done, not just thought about • practical and feasible solutions are required	• becoming totally pragmatic, expedient, and always resorting to improvised, one-off solutions • undervaluing the importance of thinking • failing to see any general patterns or to gain any insights
Planning	• you need to make plans, set goals, think about the future • you need to work out what resources you will require to meet your goals • you are preparing forecasts and budgets • you need to anticipate the consequences and effects of what you are doing	• making grandiose plans that are in fact quite impractical • spending all your time thinking about the future, thus avoiding or neglecting the present
Reviewing	• something has happened and you want to evaluate it, to see how well you are doing • you are at the end of a project or task and you want to see what you have learned from it • someone wants their performance to be appraised	• living in the past, so that you never look to the present or the future; living on past achievements, or worrying about failures and saying "if only I/we/you had..." • becoming trapped by guilt
Integrating	• all the time; being aware of what is happening around you; sensitive to the needs of the situation and the people in it; humourous and cheerful; mediating between people in conflict; balancing confrontation and support; theory and practice, past and present	• assuming that you must always be in charge • manipulating people to suit your own needs

A most useful exercise would be to give yourself points - out of 10 say - for each style. Seven times ten would be perfect - not very likely!

Then talk to friends and colleagues about it. Explain the styles to them, and ask them to score you. Compare their scores with yours, to get an idea of how they see you!

This is, of course, a special example of feedback from others, described in chapter 2. A sophisticated exercise would be to do a repertory grid (method 12), using situations when you applied each style as the examples.

It may be that certain situations or people bring out different styles in you. This could be particularly true of the style distortions. Try keeping a record of when these appear, and why. Who was involved? What was happening?

You can also seek feedback from other people about distortions. Explain what they are and ask how and when they see them appearing in your behaviour.

7.6 Suggestions for further reading

Benson, H.; Klipper, J.Z. The relaxation response. London, Collins, 1976.

Cooper, K.H. The new aerobics. New York, Bantam, 1970.

Diagram group. The complete book of exercises. London, Arrow, 1982.

Easwaran, E. The Mantram handbook. Petaluma, California, Nilgiri Press, 1977.

Feldenkrais, M. Awareness through movement. New York, Harper and Row, 1972.

Ferrucci, P. What we may be. Wellingborough, Turnstone Press, 1982.

Goleman, D. The varieties of meditative experience. New York, Dutton, 1977.

Jacobson, E. <u>Tension control for businessmen</u>. New York, McGraw-Hill, 1963.

Leshan, L. <u>How to meditate</u>. London, Sphere, 1978.

Madders, J. <u>Relax</u>. London, BBC Publications, 1973.

Schiller, P.E. <u>Rudolf Steiner and initiation</u>. New York, Anthroposophic Press, 1981.

Zeylmans van Emmichoven, F. <u>The anthroposophical understanding of the soul</u>. New York, Anthroposophic Press, 1982.

HOW OTHER PEOPLE CAN
HELP YOUR SELF-DEVELOPMENT

8

As already mentioned in chapter 1, other people can be very helpful in your self-development. Indeed, it is probably true to say that they are essential.

Perhaps the most obvious way they can help is by being supportive and listening to you talk about yourself and your development. Surprisingly, though, it is often people whom we do not like, who are not supportive, who can play an essential role in our development. This is because such people provide us with a challenge - with the opportunity to try to develop patience, tolerance, real understanding of others (it is relatively easy with people we really like).

So, although friends are indeed very important in your development, try to look on other, less pleasant, people as being "sent" to give you a developmental task to work on.

Most of our encounters with others occur as part of our everyday living. However, you may wish to establish some special developmental relationship, either individually or in groups. This chapter looks at these in detail, as follows:

(26) working with a speaking partner;

(27) group approaches.

8.1 Method 26: Working with a speaking partner

Although not essential, you can certainly stand to gain a lot by joining together with someone who is also working on his or her self-development, with the understanding that each of you will help the other.

To be effective in helping each other you and your speaking partner should agree to meet regularly. Once a week, fortnight or month are recommended. We also suggest that you fix a minimum of at least one hour (after all, that only gives you half an hour each) for the session; two hours would be better.

What do you want to talk about? All sorts of things; anything that helps your development. If you have fixed a definite programme of self-development, you can talk about your progress with that. Describe

- entries in your personal journal;

- something you have been reading;

- what happened when you tried out some personal experimentation;

- certain critical incidents;

- etc., etc.

Another way is simply to start talking about progress in general. "What is new and good in your self-development?" could be a useful - and positive - opening.

It is important to be comfortable and informal when working with a speaking partner. Usually this will involve sitting; sit so that you are directly facing each other, reasonably close. Do not have any furniture (such as a desk or table) between you.

Choosing the partner

Who might make an appropriate speaking partner? The main requirement is that he or she should be committed to working on their own development, as well as to helping you with yours! You in turn, of course, must be committed

152

to helping them. You might find a colleague or a friend who would like to join you in this venture. Perhaps, though, you may prefer someone you do not already know - in many ways, perhaps surprisingly, it is easier (at least to start off) with a comparative stranger.

The problem there, of course, is, "How do I find a comparative stranger?" You could ask your training manager, if your organisation has one. Otherwise, perhaps talking about it from time to time might bring you in touch with someone who would also be interested.

It can be very fruitful if you work together with a close member of your family, such as your wife or husband. However, it must be recognised that this is often extremely difficult, due to your involvement with each other, which tends to get in the way of objective and supportive listening.

Objective and supportive listening

For it is this process of objective and supportive listening that lies at the heart of working with a speaking partner. This is in fact a most important point. We can illustrate it by reflecting on some of your own experience.

To do this, think of three or four people who have been helpful to you in the past. Then jot down on a piece of paper, or in your personal journal (method 1), what it was about them that made them helpful. The odds are that what made them helpful included things like

- they were sympathetic;

- they showed interest in me;

- they respected me;

- they still liked me even when I made mistakes or did something stupid;

- they sometimes challenged or confronted me but in a way which showed they still respected me.

153

You may also have noted that they gave you advice. However, this one crops up surprisingly rarely. It seems as though people who are really helpful seldom give advice. And if they do, it is in such a way that we feel able to reject the advice if we so wish. In a way, it is not so much giving advice as helping us to generate our own solutions.

Here, then, is the key to the type of help we are talking about when considering joining with a speaking partner. What you should be looking for from him or her ... and what you should be offering back in turn ... includes:

- support, commitment, respect;

- listening to what the other person is thinking, feeling and willing;

- non-judgmental listening;

- empathy; a feeling that you understand how the other person feels, that you can almost feel it yourself;

- holding back on advice and on making suggestions about what the other person should or should not do (although help in generating possible solutions can be useful).

You can try to develop two types of listening pattern, and use them when appropriate. We can call these "unresponding" and "responding" listening.

In unresponding listening, the listener does not make any response to the speaker. Suppose you are the listener. Before you start, you agree a time limit - say ten minutes. Those ten minutes are for your partner to talk. You then show that you are interested and committed by looking at your partner in the face. In this way your attention remains focused on the speaker, rather than being allowed to wander off onto your own thoughts.

So, you pay close attention, and listen. You do not reply in any way. You do not say anything, or nod, or grunt or whatever. You listen. Even if the speaker pauses, or stops, you do not speak, or encourage. You just quietly remain closely attentive, waiting, listening, until the time limit (ten minutes or whatever) is up. Then you swap round.

This may sound unusual; indeed, it is unusual. It is not like our normal to and fro way of listening in everyday conversation. However, experience shows that it can be most effective in allowing the speaker really to get into the topic or issue being talked about. Merely having an attentive, supportive listener - even a seemingly inactive one - can be most helpful in allowing someone to think aloud and examine and share their thoughts, feelings and wishes.

This is particularly true during the silences. By not speaking, the listener gives the speaker time to sort things out in his or her head; to clarify ideas, to recognise feelings, to identify wishes. So, although at first it is difficult, do not be afraid of the periods of silence. Do not fall into the trap of filling them with some sort of response - although it is very often tempting to do so, to demonstrate how "helpful" you want to be.

There will, though, be times when it is useful to use responding listening. This is where the non-advice approach needs to be remembered. If advice should in general be avoided, what sort of responses are likely to be helpful?

There is in fact a simple but useful classification of listening and responding behaviours that we can apply, shown diagrammatically in figure 24. This classification is related to that used for skills of self-development, chapter 1, figure 5. Can you see the connections?

Table 11 gives a number of ways of responding in each of the seven categories. Since there is a danger at times of being over-eager to be caring, or confronting, or whatever, some cautionary remarks are also included.

You will notice that most of the ways of helping involve questions, not statements. Furthermore, the questions are what are known as "open-ended". That is, they cannot be answered by "yes" or "no", but need elaboration; they encourage your partner to talk. By the way, most of the questions in the longer questionnaires in

155

Figure 24. Seven categories of listening behaviour

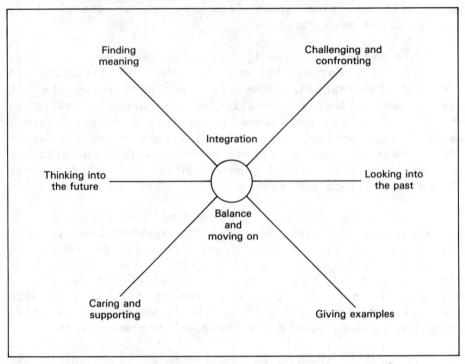

the appendices are also open-ended. You can get some idea about how to ask open-ended questions by looking over those questionnaires.

All the time, listen to what your partner is

(1) thinking:

observe what is said; pattern of thought (how logical is it?); is he/she giving overviews, or going into a lot of detail? Is it all in the past? Or present? Or future? What other people are being referred to? Who is not being referred to? What is not talked about? What imagery, or metaphors, are being used? How are sentences being put together?

(2) feeling:

look out for what is said but also, perhaps more importantly, for physical clues, such as gestures,

156

tone of voice, posture, way of breathing, manner-isms;

(3) willing:

do not forget the difference between a wish ("what I would like to do") and an intention ("what I am going to do").

If at all possible, be aware of yourself, too - what are you thinking, feeling and willing, whilst listening and talking?

Perhaps table 11 looks a bit daunting! Do not be put off. Being a skilled listener is very difficult, and takes a lot of practice. You and your speaking partner can still be very helpful to each other, long before you have mastered these questioning techniques. So although these are most useful, and you are recommended to start trying to use them, the most important thing is that you and your partner are committed to helping each other.

8.2   Method 27: Group approaches

Various trainers have devised a range of approaches to group work (e.g. T. groups, teamwork development, encounter groups, etc.). However, for self-development within organisations our experience favours the three types of group described in this section, which are usually acceptable and effective. These are action-learning groups, self-help groups and self-development groups. They are basically rather similar, so it is convenient to consider them together.

What do they have in common? First, each consists of a fairly small number of participants - usually between six and ten; about eight is probably an ideal number. They may have a professional trainer to help them (self-development groups; trainer-led, action-learning groups). Another shared feature is that they meet regularly. How often they meet depends on the wishes of participants, although approximately once a month is common. The meetings also vary in length - again according to participants' wishes, and to what is possible. Four hours would normally be considered the absolute minimum required for a meeting, although if at all possible six to seven hours should be aimed for (often the first meeting, when the group starts up, is longer - say two or three days).

157

Table 11. Some ways of helpful listening

CATEGORY	WAYS OF HELPING YOUR PARTNER	BUT, BEWARE! SOME CAUTIONARY REMARKS
GENERAL	ALL THE TIME: LISTEN TO YOURSELF AND YOUR INNER VOICE IS YOUR HIGHER OR LOWER SELF IN CHARGE?	
CARING AND SUPPORTING Showing you are interested in your partner, that you respect him or her, and that you have some degree of understanding of what they are thinking and of how they are feeling. ("Empathy"). Giving positive feedback is also involved here, as is receiving feedback.	— pay attention; face your partner, sit reasonably close and look at him or her — show that you are hearing, by nodding, smiling, using other facial expressions, saying "hmm" — make brief statements, such as: "Does that make you feel sad/excited/frightened/... whatever?" or "If I were in your position, I think that I would be feeling..." or "When that happened to me I felt..." or "I guess that makes you want to..." — if it comes naturally in your situation, it might be helpful to show that you care by some physical means, such as holding your partner's hand; putting a hand on his/her shoulder; giving a hug; or similar — give positive feedback — when receiving positive feedback, acknowledge it gracefully. Don't deny it, nor belittle it. — when receiving negative feedback, try to listen to it (even if you don't accept it). For example ● don't deny criticism ● don't be on the defensive ● don't be counter-critical or counter-attacking ● do listen and respond, using the same words even if you don't accept the judgement as such e.g. "perhaps I was rude..." "maybe I am often late..." — if you think the criticism is justified, prompt for more, e.g. "can you think of other occasions when I did that?"	— don't stare too hard, otherwise it could be off-putting — don't overdo these — you need a careful balance between interrupting too much and not saying enough — avoid statements such as "I wouldn't worry about that if I were you." Although intended to be supportive, these often give the impression that you don't really understand the speaker's problem. — avoid positive feedback being too warm and comfortable
CHALLENGING AND CONFRONTING Sometimes, a challenge or confrontation can be useful. However, try to do it in a way that shows you are not attacking your partner as a person. Giving negative feedback is also involved here.	— look out for inconsistencies or contradictions in what your partner is saying — point these out, either directly or by asking questions such as "how can you say both a and b?" or "how consistent are a and b?" — similarly, look out for any inconsistencies between your partner's words and actions (for example, saying "I am not angry" whilst shouting or hitting the table) — again, watch for inconsistencies between your partner's thoughts, apparent feelings and wishes/intentions — ask questions like "Can you be sure of what you have just said? How?" (Checking on assumptions). — highlight differences between wishes and intentions	— examine your motives for challenging. Is it to help your partner? Or to satisfy your own needs, (e.g. for power; revenge; to let off steam?) — listen to your tone of voice; observe your actions, gestures and body posture. Beware of being too aggressive, too threatening. Try to confront in a way that it is still supportive. Show you still like your partner as a person.

158

Table 11. Continued

CATEGORY	WAYS OF HELPING YOUR PARTNER	BUT, BEWARE! SOME CAUTIONARY REMARKS
	— give any negative feedback in as supportive a way as you can. For example ● make "I" statements, e.g. "I felt attacked when you..." rather than "you attacked me..." ● give 2 or 3 examples to illustrate what it is you don't like	— give feedback, not slapback. Show you still like and value your partner as a person, even if you don't like what they have done — criticise behaviour, not the person.
FINDING MEANING Interpreting what has been heappening	— ask questions like ● does this happen often? Do you think/feel this often? When? ● can you see any pattern in all this? ● what does it mean to you? ● what is this, (or this person), saying to you? ● why are these things happening to you?	— beware of imposing your interpretations or meanings on your partner's situation. — look out for rationalisations. If you hear any, consider switching to confronting.
GIVING EXAMPLES	— ask questions like ● can you give examples of what has been happening? of the sort of person you have difficulty with? of the sort of things you are afraid might happen? of the feelings you get when...?	
LOOKING INTO THE PAST	— ask questions like ● has this happend before? When? ● have you thought or felt like this before? When? What happened? ● have you wanted to do this before? When? What happened?	— avoid getting trapped in the past, e.g. saying "if only...", or unhelpful blaming.
THINKING TO THE FUTURE	— ask questions like ● what do you want to do about this? ● what will be the consequences — for you and for others? What will you and they be thinking and feeling? ● what obstacles do you forsee? What can you do about these? ● What alternatives are there?	— avoid living in the future, e.g. "it will be all right when..." (hence there is nothing to do except wait) or "I can't do anything until..." What can you do now, to help these future things?
BALANCE INTEGRATION AND MOVING ON	Basically, this involves being aware of yourself and of what is going on whilst listening — noticing your own thoughts, feelings, wishes and intentions (see also listening to yourself, method 4) — remaining objective; not allowing the way you are hearing your partner to be influenced by your own thoughts, feelings and wishes — noticing what your partner is thinking, feeling and wanting to do about the talking session itself — sensing which of the other 6 categories is needed; and switching to it — asking questions like "what shall we do now?" (i.e. what is our next step in this speaking session?") — bringing a bit of lightness into the situation, by laughing, talking about a relatively unimportant mutual interest.	— why is it needed? Whose needs will this satisfy? — don't overdo this, otherwise you will find yourself avoiding the real issues.

In each type of group, members have to decide if they are going to concentrate on work-based issues, or widen the horizons of the group and allow members to focus on any aspects of their development (work, home, family, social activities, whole of life).

Whichever they choose, there is a common process of exploring the issues, both individually and with other members, often with further individual work during the time between meetings. Each member then discusses this individual work at the next meeting, and receives comments, feedback, ideas, challenges, support and so on from the other participants.

In an action-learning group, each member takes a particular work or life issue and concentrates on it, both during the meetings and in between.

In the case of the other two types of group, a range of other strategies may be adopted. For example, members might

- carry out some self-development activities (like those in this book). They may do these together (in pairs, sub-groups or the whole group), or do them in the time between the meetings and then discuss what happened when they get together;

- choose a common theme (e.g. "listening") and work on that;

- discuss key events in their lives;

- work on mini-action learning projects, by talking about short-term personal issues;

- look at the behaviour of themselves in the group, and use this as a vehicle for development;

- do a mixture of all of these.

Each type of group has to go through a number of phases. Although it is not quite accurate to say that these follow each other in strict sequence, they more or less do occur in the following order.

160

(1) <u>Forming</u>. Recruitment to the group; establishing nature and purpose; determining frequency, place and time of meetings.

(2) <u>Trust</u>. Members growing to have confidence in each other and feeling able to talk about themselves.

(3) <u>Sense of purpose</u>. Further exploration of purpose of group; clarifying reasons why each member is there; setting some individual aims.

(4) <u>Commitment</u>. Willingness to work on your own issues, and to respect and help the other members with theirs.

(5) <u>Overall strategy</u>. From the ones described earlier.

(6) <u>Implementation of strategy</u>. Actually working on the issues, pursuing member's aims.

(7) <u>Regular review of progress</u>. How are we getting on.

(8) <u>Closing down</u>. Terminating the group in a constructive way.

(9) <u>Decision making</u>. This underpins the other phases, and is a constant issue. Working out how the group decides what to do next.

(10) <u>Basic processes</u>. Certain key processes, such as listening, understanding thinking/feeling/willing, giving and receiving feedback, are of vital importance.

Some further ideas for implementing each of these phases are given in appendix 7, intended for trainers and facilitators involved in running an action-learning or self-development group. If you are trying to set up a self-help group (without a professional trainer being present), you should also find that part very useful.

How can you decide whether or not to become involved in a group?

One of the main factors, of course, is the availability of such a group. If you work for an organisation which has a training officer or management trainer, then

161

you could ask him or her to set one up, as part of an overall management development programme. Alternatively, an outside training institution or a management association might run one.

You could try to set up your own - either a self-help group, without a professional trainer, or bringing in a trainer or consultant from somewhere else. You would need to find between five and nine other people who were prepared to commit themselves to meeting regularly, probably for a period of at least six months, possibly one or two years.

You might feel that you are not a "group" person. That is, you prefer to work on your own. Fair enough. There is nothing wrong with that. But you might like to consider the point that learning to work with others could in itself be seen as a goal for self-development. After all, managers always work with and through people!

So, these types of group are by no means essential. However, if a suitable number of managers can get together in this way, with a reasonable level of commitment, then a group can certainly provide a useful adjunct to an individual self-development programme.

8.3   Suggestions for further reading

Egan, G. The skilled helper. London, Brooks/Cole, 1975.

Megginson, D.F.; Boydell, T.H. A guide to management coaching. London, British Association for Commercial and Industrial Education, 1979.

PROMOTING MANAGEMENT SELF-DEVELOPMENT WITHIN AN ORGANISATION 9

By now it should be clear that the development needs of managers differ from person to person. Similarly, what needs to be done within an organisation to initiate and support a programme of management self-development will very much depend on the organisation itself.

Thus, we cannot give an all-purpose statement of "do this, and development will take place". However, what we can do is to provide you with some ideas for consideration within your organisation.

If you are reading this section of the book you will probably be

- a senior manager, with interest in or res- ponsibility for management development;

- a specialist in management development, training or personnel management (within the organisation);

- a manager who wants to carry out his own self-development programme, and who wants support from the organisation;

- an external specialist, such as a management trainer or consultant, who wants to set up a programme within a client organisation.

Whichever role you are in, you will find it useful to look at the question of setting up a programme from two main perspectives, namely

- the benefits to the organisation;

- motivating managers to work on their self-development.

In this chapter, then, we will look at these two perspectives, followed by an exploration of how to create a range of resources and conditions for encouraging self-development.

9.1 The role of management self-development in improving your organisation

If a scheme is to be accepted and supported, it will need to be seen in some way to improve the organisation, as well as being helpful to individual managers. Although the effects will of course vary according to circumstances, experience shows that self-development programmes can have a number of benefits for the organisation, as already mentioned in the preface to this publication.

It is increasingly being recognised that to achieve these benefits it is necessary to adopt a strategy that focuses on the real, actual problems and issues faced by both individual managers and by the organisation as a whole. This is not to say that conventional approaches have no place, but that they need to be carried out in parallel with a self-development strategy.

Matching organisational and individual development needs

We have already seen (chapter 2) how individual self-development is built on a foundation of individual self-assessment. In the organisational context, therefore, we need to look for some form of organisational diagnosis.

This opens up a whole area that is beyond the scope of this book. However, almost as a summary, we can give some guidelines.

When diagnosing organisational needs, it is useful to have some form of framework both for data collection and for subsequent analysis. A simple framework that is often used in organisations adopting a self-development approach is shown in table 12, which suggests focusing on four main

Table 12. Organisational diagnosis checklist

Aspects of the organisation	Things to consider: What is good or bad? What needs changing or developing?
IDENTITY	- overall essence of the organisation; - cultural values (traditions, norms, practices; - overall managerial ideology - the way decisions are made (according to needs of powerful bosses, of rules and procedures, of the task in hand, or of each individual);
RELATIONSHIPS	- style of leadership; - functions and roles; the way these are allocated, and extent to which they are understood; - relationships between groups and departments; - relationships within groups and departments; - relationships with clients, customers, owners, general public.
PROCESSES	- production, manufacturing, and service processes; - administrative processes; - systems; - decision making; - training and learning; - nature, frequency and quality of meetings; - information flow.
PHYSICAL AND MATERIAL RESOURCES	- equipment, tools, machinery; - rooms, space; - climate, environment.

aspects of the organisation. Some useful ways of obtaining relevant data about these various aspects are briefly summarised in appendix 5.

Obviously every organisation is in many ways unique, and will face its own particular problems and developmental issues. You will need to be working at identifying and recognising these continuously.

At the same time, though, it might be useful to bear in mind some typical problems and issues that have been found to arise in most organisations. These aspects of the organisation (mainly related to its size and age), are shown in table 13. You can use this table as a general guide when working with your organisation's issues, and when trying to integrate these with the development needs of individual managers. In this way, the issues will influence the resources provided, the processes introduced, the relationship work and the goals and policies you establish.

Figure 25 shows the overall process of organisational analysis. Data about the four aspects (table 12), together with issues arising from the organisation's phase of development (table 13), are brought together. Much of these data will be threatening and disturbing to various people, and it is important that efforts are made to work on the data in a manner which recognises this, and which resolves any conflicts that may well arise at this stage.

If this is done, a number of questions and issues facing the organisation will be identified. These then need to be discussed with managers, exploring what people think, feel, and want to do about them. At this point, too, questions of individual self-development can come into the discussion.

The outcomes from this will probably be a number of priorities and plans for a programme that will provide ideas and suggestions for the self-development of managers, and enhance the development of the organisation itself.

166

Figure 25. The process of organisational analysis

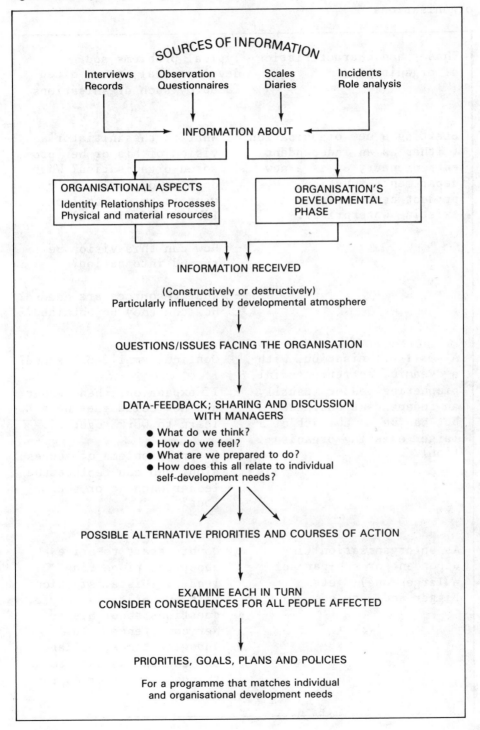

SOURCES OF INFORMATION

Interviews   Observation   Scales   Incidents
Records   Questionnaires Diaries   Role analysis

INFORMATION ABOUT

ORGANISATIONAL ASPECTS

Identity Relationships Processes
Physical and material resources

ORGANISATION'S
DEVELOPMENTAL
PHASE

INFORMATION RECEIVED

(Constructively or destructively)
Particularly influenced by developmental atmosphere

QUESTIONS/ISSUES FACING THE ORGANISATION

DATA-FEEDBACK; SHARING AND DISCUSSION
WITH MANAGERS

● What do we think?
● How do we feel?
● What are we prepared to do?
● How does this all relate to individual
  self-development needs?

POSSIBLE ALTERNATIVE PRIORITIES AND COURSES OF ACTION

EXAMINE EACH IN TURN
CONSIDER CONSEQUENCES FOR ALL PEOPLE AFFECTED

PRIORITIES, GOALS, PLANS AND POLICIES

For a programme that matches individual
and organisational development needs

167

Table 13. Developmental issues typically faced by organisations

Phases and characteristics of organisations	Typical problems and developmental issues often faced by such organisations
Starting a new organisation (either as an independent entrepreneur, or as a new department, function, product centre within an existing enterprise).	– What is the initiator's vision of his or her proposed organisation? What does he or she ideally want it to do, to look like, to feel like? – How can this vision be turned into action? – What resources are needed? How can they be obtained?
A small organisation, with a dynamic, entrepreneurial, pioneering leader (usually an independent business, but can be a new part of a larger existing organisation).	– Continue small, or expand? – If expansion, then leader and new colleagues need to learn to work together. – Later, problems of succession. Who can replace the leader when he or she goes?
As an organisation (independent or sub-part of a larger one), gets bigger and more complex.	– Doubts start to arise about the pioneering leader. Dissatisfaction with authoritarian style, questions about his or her competence. In changing times, reliance on "the way we used to do things" no longer appropriate.

Table 13. (continued)

Phases and characteristics of organisations	Typical problems and developmental issues often faced by such organisations
	– A need arises to bring order into chaos, with systematic scientific management, with logical planning implementation and control.
	– This can be done by standardisation, rules, procedures, job descriptions.
	– At the same time specialist functions are established (e.g. sales, administration, research, personnel).
An organisation that has had this logical, scientific management approach for some time	– Problems of rigidity, bureaucracy set in.
	– Reduced motivation; apathy.
	– Competition and rivalry between different parts of the organisation.
	– Need for social skills training, teamwork development, opportunities for individual development, to overcome these problems.

Table 13. (continued)

Phases and characteristics of organisations	Typical problems and developmental issues often faced by such organisations
An organisation that has lost touch with the outside world (this often happens as organisations get older and bigger especially in the case of bureaucracies).	- Continuing need for improved, flexible, developmental, internal, relationships. - Need to change relationship with customers and clients. To move from unhealthy view (they are seen almost as "enemies" who have to be cajoled, bullied, tricked) to healthy one (seen as collaborators, partners in a mutually advantageous venture). - Similar changes need to be made in relationship with other external stakeholders (e.g. owners, government, local community).
A dying organisation (i.e. one that has either failed to the point of bankruptcy, or whose initial mission is no longer valid or viable.	- Can anything be done to reverse the failure or to acquire a new mission, a new vision, and hence start again? - If not, what can be done to make the closing down process as positive and painless as possible? What are the moral obligations to the various stakeholders (employees, owners, customers community?).

Clearly, when establishing priorities, goals, plans and policies, you will need to consider other implications of the development, including those for equipment and processes, as well as for other aspects of the human resources development and management, such as recruitment, remuneration or formal training.

Developmental atmosphere or climate

You will see from figure 25 that the extent to which the information will be handled constructively or destructively (i.e. responded to by the organisation's higher or lower self, in the terms of chapter 2) is especially influenced by the nature of the "developmental atmosphere" within the organisation.

This atmosphere is a general feeling, within the organisation, arising particularly as a result of the developmental aspects of its relationships and of its identity.

It is a significant decision of your organistion's internal "culture", which may be either development and change oriented, or conservative and essentially negative to attempts to change the status quo, and to various initiatives taken or suggested by individual managers and workers.

There is no quick way of improving these - of making them positive, helpful for development. However, as a start you might like to think about the predominant management style (see chapter 7). How helpful is this? Is there anything you can do to improve it?

Changing the predominant style will, of course, not be at all easy. It might be possible, over quite a long period of time, by management skills, training, discussions, teamwork development programmes, role clarification and negotiation exercises, and other ways of helping people to give and receive feedback about how they see each other. But we would be deluding ourselves if we thought this would be anything but a lengthy and difficult process.

That is not to say, though, that you should not try. Far from it. But we are sorry to say that you should not expect a painless, effortless path to instant success, using a magical technique. You will have to keep at it for quite a long time, often in the face of disappointments, discouragements, or even downright hostility and opposition. But it can work and it is working, slowly but surely, in a whole variety of organisations in different parts of the world.

A very good start is by making people aware of what is currently going on, of the present situation. You can do a data feedback exercise by systematically finding out what others actually do think and feel, and then giving them a summary of this information in written form (a report), or through a series of meetings and discussions.

There are various ways of obtaining this information. One would be to go round talking with managers, asking how they see and experience things. This has the advantage of being participative, but it would also be very time-consuming. An alternative would be to ask managers to complete a questionnaire (see appendix 6).

All these, of course, are internal relationships. External relationships can also be supportive and developmental, such as with local colleges, community groups, professional bodies, colleagues in other organisations.

A very significant way of building developmental relationships is through the use of special development groups. This term covers the three types of group already described in chapter 8. Just to recapitulate, these are action-learning groups, self-development groups, and self-help groups.

Groups can be set up for managers from one particular organisation; alternatively, you can arrange an "all comers" group. It is useful to have a range of ages and levels of seniority, although sometimes it can be difficult if an immediate boss and subordinate are in the same group. Groups of this nature can also be useful for specific sets of managers (e.g. those on a correspondence course; newly appointed; women; about to retire). Detailed guidelines on how to manage such groups are in appendix 7.

Figure 26. Stakeholders in a self-development programme

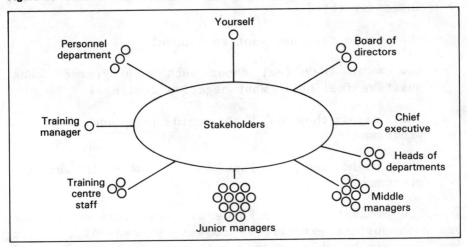

Experience has shown that numerous benefits arise from such groups. These benefits have been found to be both for the individuals taking part (greater skills, awareness, understanding, etc.) and, equally important, for their organisations.

9.2 Motivating people for a programme of management self-development

If you want people to support and participate in a programme of management self-development, you will have to ensure that they see some benefit in it for themselves, as well as for the organisation. In fact, we have already noted (figure 25) that the planning discussions should set out to relate organisational and individual needs.

Stakeholders in a self-development programme

It is helpful at this point to consider the various people (as well as yourself) who are likely to be involved in, and affected by, a self-development programme. You can draw up a diagram like figure 26 which is merely an example; your own diagram should include relevant people - or groups - from your own organisation.

When you have identified these key people (or groups), you can then start to think about the ways in which they might affect the programme. In each case, try to identify:

- what would they like a programme to achieve? What is in it for them?

- what would they not want to happen?

- how would they feel about such a programme? What positive feelings? What negative feelings?

- what might they do that would help and support a programme?

- what might they do that would hinder or weaken a programme?

You probably will not have all this information yet, and an important exercise is to set up means of obtaining it. You may be able to talk with many of those involved, but, more probably, it will be better to initiate an organisation-wide discussion of the whole programme.

How you do this will depend on the methods of briefing and opinion-seeking that are feasible within your organisation. These might include

- briefing meetings (information given to heads of departments, who then brief their subordinates);

- special meetings with groups of managers;

- special short workshops;

- regular individual appraisal sessions;

- briefing by written memoranda.

Whichever method you use, your aim will be to explore the link between organisational and individual needs, and ways in which a programme of self-development can help to meet these needs.

At times, of course, you might come across some managers who are sceptical or even hostile. The best way to deal with this is probably by individual counselling, but you may find it helpful to recall some of the benefits that have been experienced by managers who carry out self-development programmes, including:

174

- learning new skills;

- improved job performance;

- making the best of themselves;

- career progression;

- self-satisfaction;

- greater recognition.

You may also come across other obstacles. For example, there may be jealousy from people who feel that others are getting unfair special attention; vested interests (e.g. in other forms of management training) may be threatened. And so on.

Noting the thoughts and feelings of the various stakeholders will at least be a first step in resolving these issues, although obviously you will then need to engage in considerable talk and discussion to sort them out.

This will mean, then, that you will somehow have to involve individual managers in identifying their own needs. Obviously, many of the ways described in this book (chapter 2 and various appendices) can be used for this, either by simply giving them to managers or by combining them with some of the briefing methods just mentioned. A general questionnaire for use with a large number of managers, thereby getting an overall picture of organisation-wide individual needs, is shown in appendix 8.

The influence of age on the developmental issues of managers

Obviously, the needs of the various managers will to a considerable extent depend on the individuals concerned - on their particular strengths, weaknesses, interests and so on.

However, it has been shown that, as managers grow older, they tend to face certain typical age-related developmental issues in addition to their particular ones. That is, there is a link between a manager's age and his or her development.

Some of these age-related concerns as perceived by a number of European organisations, will now be examined. They may need some modification to bring them into line with what happens in a local culture. However, we hope that they might serve as a basis for working with managers in your organisation on the issues of their self-development.

Early and middle twenties (21-28)

Young managers are entering the world, finding their feet. They want to find out about themselves, what they can do, how they are getting on; they need to be noticed. They therefore need considerable variety of experience - avoiding early specialisation - complete with regular, frequent feedback.

Late twenties to middle thirties (28-35)

Now more confident, managers in this age group need to deepen their relationships with their work (and with people). This should therefore be a time for specialisation and increased responsibility. This is also a period of analytical, rational and logical thinking. Therefore analytical tasks are particularly appropriate, involving objective reflection and planning. They can also be encouraged to take a similar approach to planning their own lives - taking the initiative in analysing their aims, activities, strengths and weaknesses, and planning for the future.

Middle thirties to early forties

Often a turbulent period, with recurring doubts about themselves and what they have been doing. "What is the point of this sort of work?" is a common cry; "The thought of another 20 years doing this is enough to make me go mad". They may need help to manage these feelings - which, incidentally, are often denied or suppressed, being hidden by great bursts of frenzied activity, or somewhat frantic (and often unfortunate) changes in job or life-style. There is a need to take stock, to take a detailed look at their life so far, trying to make meaning of the past and present, as a platform on which to build the future. Sharing the problems, counselling, group work (including biography), can all be useful here. The aim is

176

to try to answer questions such as "what is really important to you now? What do you want to do? In what ways can
you see the organisation developing, and what opportunities will this offer? What new overviews can you open
up? How can you make things more interesting, challenging, satisfying?"

Middle and late forties

From now on, much depends on the extent to which the
35-42 period was successfully managed. If the storm was
weathered well, then this next period can become the start
of a new enthusiasm. There is less need to achieve, to do
well, to be a success. Instead there is a desire to do
something useful, to make a contribution to the organisation, to others, to the community. It is almost as if
up until now the manager has been taking, and he or she
wants to start giving something back. They may require
help in deciding what it is they have to give, what they
can contribute in their own unique way. For those who
were unable to come to grips with the earlier crisis,
however, there is often a deepening problem, characterised
by becoming hard, defensive, cynical, arrogant, domineer-
ing - generally unpleasant to be with! They will need
much help to overcome this - not so much by being directly
confronted, but by being helped to see what they are doing
and the effect this is having on others around them. Both
groups will also need to start to come to terms with the
fact that they will not live for ever - although it is
likely that the first group will find this easier to
accept than the others.

Fifties (49-56)

By now, those who successfully matured will be
capable of making a valuable contribution to the organisation and to others, by developing out of their experience
a mixture of wisdom, compassion, and real skill in dealing
with other people. They should be given every opportunity
to use those abilities. Those who have not yet conquered
their doubts and fears, however, will continue to be
negative and difficult to work with. Consideration might
be given to keeping them away from other people on whom
they might have a damaging and demoralising effect; for
example, they might be moved to specialised but narrow
work areas. However, they may still benefit from support

and counselling. At this age, too, serious consideration needs to be given to physical and health issues.

Approaching retirement

There are now two main issues - handing over what you know to someone else, and preparing to retire. Those who matured successfully will find both of these much easier than the others, who are more likely to view the whole prospect as a tremendous threat. In so doing, they may well deny the impending change, or avoid thinking about it at all. This means, of course, that they will be reluctant to do anything about preparing others for their job. When the actual day comes, they are likely to be at a loss. It is therefore important to help people in this age group to explore alternative post-retirement activities.

Management policy for encouraging self-development

All in all, people in the organisation must feel that self-development is not regarded as solely their private matter, but as an effort that is wanted and appreciated by management. Individuals who engage in self-development programmes often have to make a greater effort than many of their colleagues, and devote a considerable part of their private leisure time to this. They must see that such an effort and sacrifice pays off in terms of job content, career, remuneration, new opportunities for learning and the like. Management has to provide its support to self-development both in individual cases (helping individuals to draw up and carry out a programme that makes sense both from the individual's and the organisation's point of view) and in general policy terms (policy declarations, availability of resources, suggesting examples of individuals to be followed by others and the like).

9.3 Creating resources and conditions for self-development

We will now examine some of the resources and activities whereby you can help self-development to take place within your organisation.

178

Material and physical resources

What kind of materials could you make available for managers to use for self-development?

Perhaps the most obvious are books; some form of internal library - even quite an informal one - can be set up. The nature of the books will depend on your circumstances. Over 400 book titles are described in the Self-development bibliography. This could give you a good idea of the range of books available. There are, of course, a smaller number of references in this book itself. Perhaps these could form the nucleus of a useful collection.

As well as books, it can be very useful if you subscribe to some journals. Not only can these play a valuable part in keeping people up to date, but managers might be encouraged to write for them as a developmental activity. Also, there is a rapidly increasing number of local journals being published, which are more likely to be directly appropriate for local circumstances than are some of the foreign books.

Less formal publications, such as relevant papers and reports, can also be collected together and made available.

A specific type of publication - known as a package - is worthy of special mention. Some packages come in book form (indeed, in many ways this book is itself a package). Others are in loose-leaf binders, or similar formats. Many packages include audio-visual material.

The main characteristic of a package is that it includes materials and exercises for the managers actually to use, to do something with. The main disadvantage of commercially produced packages is that they are usually prepared for European or American cultures. Large organisations might be able to produce packages appropriate for their own particular circumstances; alternatively, national institutions could very usefully prepare or modify packages that are suitable for local organisations.

You can also put together less formal collections of useful exercises, activities, checklists and guidance materials, using a simple filing system. Although lacking the overall cohesive structure of a package as such, this type of collection can be extremely useful.

It is useful to maintain an up-to-date collection of brochures and prospectuses on courses, to show what is available, what entry requirements are imposed, how much they cost.

Turning to modern technology, a number of computer programmes are becoming available that are designed for self-development. Before investing in this potentially expensive area, however, you would be well advised to study the features of alternative systems carefully.

Finally, another extremely important material resource is space - room or rooms where managers can spend some quiet time working on their development, either individually or in groups. Although this can be done in ordinary offices, it is very likely that they will be interrupted. So a few rooms - or just one if that is all that is possible - with no interruptions, comfortable (not luxurious) furniture, and air-conditioning if necessary, can be extremely useful. The general environment (temperature, noise, humidity) can also influence one's ability to learn and develop.

Introducing developmental processes

By "developmental processes" we mean various things that can be done to help development to take place.

One whole set of processes is using the developmental materials that were discussed in the previous section. So you can encourage managers to read the books, do the activities in the packages (including this book itself), and so on.

You will have to decide how to "encourage them". To some extent this will depend on the support you have for self-development - how keen the managers are. You may also have to brief people, train them one might say, as to what is available and how to use it. We will return to this later in the chapter.

In chapter 8 we looked at ways to self-development involving other people. An important helping activity is therefore putting people in touch with one another. A management trainer, for example, is often at the centre of a network of people interested in development. He can therefore be in a position to know of people who might be helpful for each other. Perhaps a particular manager wants to learn some specific technical knowledge - then put him in touch with a colleague who knows a lot about that topic. Alternatively, managers who are interested in a common topic or issue can be introduced to each other for the mutual exchange of ideas, or to set up a group (chapter 8). Or it may be that someone is having diffi- culty at work - again, arrange a meeting with another manager who is good at that sort of thing. Ideally, of course, people will seek out others on their own initiat- ive. However, they may well need assistance in doing so at first, followed by encouragement to do so independently.

This leads us into the area of coaching and counselling - which is what those meetings would involve. Some of the skills required for these vital processes are described in chapter 8.

Coaching and counselling really can be quite fundamental in an overall programme of self-development. For example, they can be used

- to meet specific needs for knowledge and skills;

- to help on particular difficulties; turning problems and crises into opportunities for development;

- as a part of appraisal systems;

- as an adjunct to other developmental activities, e.g. when someone returns from a course, or after they carry out some other developmental exercise or activity;

- when someone is faced with new tasks (e.g. on transfer or secondment).

As well as at times providing specific knowledge or guidance, counselling is a major vehicle for helping the manager to reflect on his or her experience - a core development process, as discussed in chapter 1. Equally important, it provides the necessary support and confrontation, associated with the skills and qualities required for development.

As well as making contacts, networking can include passing on information. For example, a management trainer can act almost as an internal "talent scout", looking out for vacancies and for people in other parts of the company who might be considered for internal transfer to make better use of their skills. Again, you can help managers contact others who have been on a particular course, or used a package, to give their opinions on it.

A definite system of such transfers, job rotation, secondments and short-term projects can be very developmental.

Similar processes include membership of special working parties and committees, visits to consumers, clients, customers, suppliers, and attachments to outside bodies, such as community organisations. This last method is growing in popularity, as organisations realise that not only can it be very developmental for the manager concerned, but it also fulfils a very real need in the local society.

Another form of outside body is the professional institution. Managers can be encouraged to join these and take an active part in their activities. Offering local branches the use of your facilities for meetings (e.g. rooms and equipment) is likely to help here.

We must not forget to mention the provision of courses as a self-development process. Large organisations may run their own, but more often, perhaps, managers will attend external courses.

What sort of short courses are relevant? Obviously, it depends on the needs of the people concerned. However, you might arrange - or seek - courses on

- technical aspects of the job;

- managerial skills;

- personal qualities required to be an effective manager.

This book can form the basis of some of these courses, which can incorporate many of the exercises and activities. You will notice that some of these courses can be part of the more conventional system of formal training - the main difference being the part that managers themselves play in deciding what training to undergo. Thus, self-development and formal training can - indeed should - complement each other.

Another strategy is to include self-development activities on other courses. Since this is more likely to be done by outside agencies (e.g. institutions), a fuller description of this approach is given in chapter 10. You may very well want to run some special courses on self-development, as part of an overall programme of briefing and implementation. Some ideas are provided in appendix 9.

Another very useful strategy is to establish an appropriate appraisal system. In chapter 2 we looked at the difference between appraisal by others and self-appraisal, and concluded that appraisal by others is not usually very developmental. However, an alternative is to try to synthesise the two, into a form of joint appraisal, in which the manager is helped by somebody else.

You will probably have to decide whether or not the appraisal interview is linked with salary review. Since the intention is to encourage managers to talk openly about not only their strengths, but also their weaknesses, making it part of the salary process might well inhibit them. For this reason, too, although the other appraiser may well be the immediate boss, there can be advantages in it being someone slightly removed from the direct chain of command, such as a senior manager in another department, or a training specialist. These can bring an element of neutrality into the situation, which may be helpful. On the other hand, of course, the immediate superior is usually the person who has a lot of information about the individual's performance.

Another policy question that you will need to think about here is whether to keep formal records of the appraisal. If so, what information is actually written down? Again, managers may feel inhibited if they believe that an account of their weaknesses is going to be recorded in their personal files. Perhaps a suitable compromise would be to note that the appraisal had taken place, comment on the positive strengths that were discussed, and record the action steps that were mutually agreed.

How might the appraisal be structured? One way is simply to review performance over the past six or 12 months. Another is to get both parties to complete some form of questionnaire. For example, one large organisation uses a version of the qualities of an effective manager questioned (appendix 2) adapted to its needs. Instead of a questionnaire as such, the managers rate themselves on a three point scale (high, medium or low) against each of 12 qualities. The appraiser does the same (i.e. rates the manager) and they then meet to discuss their ratings and explore both strengths and areas for improvement.

Whatever method is used, it is important to make it a positive experience. Where weaknesses are highlighted, these should be seen as opportunities for improvement and development, rather than as hideous incurable faults. The discussion should conclude with some agreement as to what needs improving, and what can be done by both parties to help with this improvement. Planning appropriate helping action will often involve finding out what is possible and feasible, which will take a bit of time. So one "appraisal episode" may well involve a series of actual meetings and discussions.

9.4 Suggestions for further reading

Boydell, T.H. A Guide to the identification of training needs. London, British Association for Commercial and Industrial Education, 1976, (2nd ed.).

Boydell, T.H.; Pedler, M.J. Management self-development bibliography. Bradford, MCB, 1979.

Boydell, T.H.; Pedler, M.J. Management self-development concepts and practices. Aldershot, Gower, 1981.

Fordyce, J.K.; Weil, R. Managing with people. Addison-Wesley, 1971.

Francis, D.; Woodcock, M. People at work. La Jolla, University Associates, 1975.

Lievegoed, B. Phases. London, Rudolf Steiner Press, 1979.

184

Lievegoed, B. The developing organization. Millbrae, California, Celestial Arts, 1980.

Management self-development: A practical manual for organisations and trainers. Sheffield, Manpower Services Commission, 1981.

Peters, T.J.; Waterman, R.H. In search of excellence. New York, Harper and Row, 1982.

Rubin, I.M.; Plovnick, M.; Fry, R. Task oriented team development package. Massachusetts Institute of Technology, 1976.

Thakur, M.; Bristow, J; Carby, K. (eds.). Personnel in change. London, Institute of Personnel Management, 1978. (Especially the chapter by Marjo van Boeschoten.)

Sperry, L.; Mickelson, D.J.; Hunsaker, P.L. You can make it happen. Reading, Massachusetts, Addison Wesley, 1977.

WHAT CAN INSTITUTIONS DO TO ENCOURAGE SELF-DEVELOPMENT? 10

So far we have concentrated on individuals and on organisations employing managers. In this chapter we will look at the ways in which management institutions can encourage and support management self-development.

There are, of course, various sorts of management institutions. They run different types of programmes and serve different sectors and levels of management. Some specialise in training, others provide a wider range of services, including research, consulting, and so on.

This chapter is not intended for one specific type of management institution. Its purpose is to give a number of specific ideas and suggestions on what an institution can do. It will be up to you to decide what your particular institution should do and how you should use self-development to enhance the quality of your programmes and services, and to help your clients in a new area.

10.1 The institution's philosophy and policy

First of all, it is useful to look at the relation-ship of self-development to your institution's management development philosophy, and to your objectives. Is the concept of self-development, as described in this book, in accordance with what you are trying to achieve? Can the practical impact of your programmes be increased if you start promoting the idea of self-development? Can you include specific self-development improvements in your programmes? Will your staff agree to this and will they follow you in your effort to enhance the "self-development dimension" of your activities?

These and similar questions have to be asked. For example, some teachers and trainers may feel that a management institution has nothing to do with manager self-development and that increased emphasis on self-development would be self-defeating, since it would reduce the demand for the institution's services. It may be useful to have a discussion with your professional staff on what self-development really means, how it can be harmonised with other activities of your institution, and how it can enhance the effects obtained through training seminars, consulting assignments, action research, action learning and other intervention methods used by your institution.

At some point you may find it useful to define your attitude to self-development, and the roles your institution wants to play in it, as a policy. Of course, such policy declaration would remain on paper if you did not help your staff in applying it in their particular activities.

Also, you can regard self-development not merely as something that is good for your clients - individual managers and management teams in organisations. Your own staff can benefit a great deal from it! In general, self-development can be of considerable help in improving the training of management teachers, trainers, consultants and researchers. Also, members of your staff will find it easier to encourage and support management self-development if they practise it themselves.

10.2 Teaching and training activities

The main teaching and training activities that you will be involved in as an institution will be those of helping people to use self-development materials, running courses, and individual counselling.

For our purposes here we can divide courses into four categories, namely:

- short introductory courses on self-development (1 day);

- longer course (say 5 days) on self-development;

- short courses on specific aspects of self-development;

- other courses, involving self-development as a process and method.

In appendix 9 there is an outline for two of these short courses (1 and 5 days) on self-development.

When it comes to specific aspects of self-development, a whole host of courses can be mounted. For example, each of chapters 4 to 8 provides a grouping of themes or topics that could form the focus of a course - built around the activities described.

Introducing self-development into existing programmes can be very helpful, especially as this may well be more acceptable to managers who might be somewhat doubtful or sceptical about a course that was specifically aimed at self-development.

How might this be done? Experience suggests two ways. The first is to include a number of sessions on self-development (e.g. based on activities in this book) amongst a number of other, subject-matter oriented sessions. At the same time, a subject-based course can be used as an opportunity for particular managers to develop by asking one or two to run one or more of the sessions, based on their specific area of expertise. Obviously, though, you will need to think about working with them on preparing their session, possibly giving some coaching on basic principles and skills of instruction.

Another way is to incorporate self-development processes into the teaching of other, subject-matter oriented sessions. This can be done by

- relating the subject matter to participant's own real life issues, by getting them to start with the issues and then helping them with theories and syllabus items. This inevitably requires a much higher level of flexibility than is usually found on content-oriented courses;

- providing a friendly learning climate, encouraging learners to take risks, disclose uncertainties; make

189

it clear that mistakes are both necessary and expected;

- encouraging a many-sided approach to issues and problems;

- helping learners to use creative thought processes, by stimulating them to look for unusual and unexpected ideas and solutions;

- using a questioning approach and encouraging participants to do the same; questioning should be open-ended and meaningful, and should cause the learner to think and explore ideas, rather than merely recite facts and definitions;

- emphasising a learning approach that views problems, issues, theories and ideas as a whole, in totality, rather than in separate, compartmentalised fragments;

- creating an atmosphere of self-evaluation, leading to self-responsibility for learning and feelings of self-worth.

Example from Nigeria

On a particular management course in Nigeria, participants (from several organisations) were asked to identify the main things that went wrong in their organisations. They shared this with each other, and it was then compared with a related theoretical model.

This process, which was used a lot during the course, included the following four steps:

(1) think about a real issue, of importance to self;

(2) share and discuss this with other participants;

(3) compare with theoretical inputs into the course (by the teacher, read in books, etc.);

(4) work out implications for self.

Whilst not entirely "self-developmental", this does compare quite well with the self-development cycle described in chapter 1 (figure 3).

During the same course, participants were also given the opportunity of doing some of the self-assessment activities from chapter 2, as well as a number of the self-development activities.

This mixture, of clear self-development sessions with other "content" ones that were handled using developmental processes, certainly led to excellent results. A formal evaluation was carried out. When asked what were the main things they had learned, participants' responses included

- I have realised that most of the things we do are related to one another and cannot be separated;

- the course is entirely different from any I have attended previously in that I feel more involved by doing a lot of thinking for myself;

- it is interesting and encouraging to note that most of my colleagues have the same problems as I have;

- I have got more confidence in talking to people in discussion; how to learn, think and understand other people's problems better;

- I have learned to think for myself;

- I now know how to be part of an organisation;

- I realise for the first time the importance of myself as a middle manager;

- I see that in an organisation, if something affects one section the others will also be affected;

- I have learned that I can make better decisions if I face problems without fear and with confidence;

- I have learned to learn by myself without necessarily having to be told everything I need to know, which I find rather stimulating and practical;

- I have come to recognise that "self" must be included when dealing with other people's shortcomings and achievements.

191

Participants were also asked what features of the course helped them to learn. The mixture of self-learning and inputs related to their own issues comes through as being central here. In particular this was achieved thanks to:

- the fact that ideas put forward by participants were accepted and respected by the tutors;

- pairing and small group work developed a strong team spirit;

- learning processes related to the participants' own experience;

- an extensive use of handouts, charts, diagrams;

- practical activities;

- a friendly atmosphere;

- relevance.

A process such as used in this case is almost bound to lead to relevance, since it starts with participants' issues.

In summary, then, this approach provides a useful - and acceptable - bridge between purely self-development activities and ordinary syllabus-content courses.

Correspondence courses

If your institution runs a correspondence programme this will require another form of teaching. Obviously these will include marking assignments and sending out new materials; other processes have been examined already, including radio or TV programmes; counselling facilities, individually or in groups; and two-way communication.

You may also like to consider the possibility of occasionally bringing together participants in a correspondence programme, for short residential workshops (say between 2 and 5 days). Obviously, one purpose for this is to give the learners an opportunity to discuss difficulties and problems with tutors. Another very important aspect of such seminars is that learners can meet each other, share experiences, and perhaps arrange to meet or correspond with each other afterwards. This can be most helpful, since one of the biggest difficulties encountered by correspondence course students is the sense of isolation.

Another way of overcoming this, and of helping learners with difficulties, would be to establish special self-development or self-help groups for correspondence course students, as well as other groups for managers working on their self-development.

10.3 Research and advice

An institution interested in promoting self-development can play a valuable role in carrying out investigations and giving advice to organisations, managers and other institutions.

For example, you might make a survey to find out what materials and resources are available and, conversely, what materials need obtaining or developing. More basic research can give valuable insights into the preparation of materials for local use, whilst evaluation research can show how effective the materials are, what difficulties or gaps are being experienced, and how things can be improved.

Similarly, an institution can both identify needs for developmental courses, and evaluate courses that are being run.

Obviously there is a wide variety of methods that could be used for identifying developmental needs. One way is to distribute a check list to a good sample of managers, and simply ask them to tick those items that they would like to improve. Appendix 8 shows such a check list, based on the outcomes of the various exercises and activities of chapters 3 to 8. The managers are asked to score each item first for its relevance to their jobs, then for the extent to which they feel they have already developed that quality or ability. You can, of course, leave out some of the items if you think they are inappropriate.

Table 14. Design for a development evaluation questionnaire

ASPECT OF DEVELOPMENT	ON THE SCALE, MARK 'B' WHERE YOU THINK YOU WERE BEFORE (THE COURSE, PACKAGE, EXPERIENCE etc.), AND 'A' WHERE YOU THINK YOU ARE NOW. (5—fully developed this aspect; 4—well developed this aspect; 3—somewhat developed this aspect; 2—not developed much of this aspect; 1—hardly developed any of this aspect). In the space between each scale, please describe briefly what, if anything, it was about (the course, package, experience etc.) that helped you to develop in this way.
list here the various aspects, as e.g. in appendix 8 (or select those you are particularly interested in)	⌊___⌋___⌋___⌋___⌋ 1 2 3 4 5 (leave approximately 2 cm between each scale)

Instruments of this nature are quite quick and simple both to administer, complete, and analyse. You can base it on any model of developmental characteristics that you like to work with. A more open-ended approach is to ask a sample of managers to write a short essay on "ways in which I would like to learn and develop", or a similar title. This, however, requires much more co-operation from the respondents, and is also more difficult to analyse. More time-consuming still - but possibly very useful - is to interview a sample of managers, individually or in groups. You can devise your own interview schedule, although open-ended questionnaires such as those in the appendices can very readily be turned into interview guidelines. Similarly, you can base an interview on the exercises for getting feedback from others, and for analysing critical incidents - both of which are also described in the appendices.

What about methods of evaluation? Again, you can either use questionnaires or interviews. A questionnaire design is shown in table 14, which is again based on the model of developmental characteristics. You will notice that it also includes space for people to describe what it was that led to the development. The questionnaire can be completed by managers who have used any of the processes or resources described in this book. Similarly, you can interview a sample of these managers.

An institution can also play a very useful research function in finding out about the nature of developmental processes that are appropriate for local culture and circumstances. Although we cannot go into this in detail, we can at least point it out as something that needs vigorous studying. A number of possible strategies might be tried, but a good starting point might be in-depth interviews with managers about the way they think they have developed over a period of time - indeed, a more detailed version of the first exercise in this book (figure 2). There is also a link here with the evaluation research, particularly if managers are again interviewed about why various processes were or were not helpful.

Information on appropriate local developmental processes can then be used for the design and implementation of materials and processes.

All this information can be made available to trainers in organisations and in other institutions, either by short courses, seminars and workshops, or through some form of bulletin or other publication.

10.4 Developmental materials and physical resources

The shortage of appropriate training and other materials is one of the biggest obstacles to self-development. This shortage is particularly acute in developing countries and generally in places that are far from industrial, administrative, and educational centres.

In this area, management institutions can play a particularly useful, though not spectacular, role.

Libraries of self-development materials

As a start you can establish a library of books, reports, periodicals, training packages, bibliographies and other materials needed for self-development. Most management institutions have a library and make it available both to staff and to course participants. Building a library for wider use in self-development processes is not the same thing. For example, you may have to establish a service providing advice to managers on what materials to choose, and also make sure that you have a sufficient number of copies of materials that will be in great demand.

Producing self-development materials

A collection of self-development materials acquired from other countries and institutions can be very useful. An even more valuable contribution could be made if your institution produces some materials of its own, adapted to the specific conditions in which your clients (managers and organisations) live, work and learn. In some cases this might be achieved by modifying existing materials that are intended for adaptation by local professional institutions. These materials may even include guidelines on feasible ways of adapting them to varying conditions (sectoral, cultural, etc.).

Materials for correspondence courses and self-development packages

As already discussed in chapter 6, a special case of structured material provision is the correspondence course. This requires a careful identification of objectives, with materials prepared to meet those objectives. The preparation of materials is a specialist subject in itself, that would need a whole book devoted to it. However, as a brief introduction we can make a few points here.

It almost goes without saying that the material should be presented in a logical sequence. However, this is not in itself sufficient. For example, it is essential that you bear the readers in mind, and write in a style that they will find acceptable. This often means leaving out certain erudite asides that might be found interesting by a different group of readers (e.g. fellow academics), but that will only confuse the learners for whom the material is primarily intended.

It is also helpful to show where one set of information relates to other parts, both things that went before, and others yet to come.

A good package, or correspondence course, is not the same as a textbook. A textbook gives a lot of relevant facts, but it is not designed to guide or teach, since it is normally used by a teacher or instructor. A package or correspondence course has to include "the teacher" within it, and therefore must do each of the following:

- arouse attention and motivate;

- make the reader aware of expected outcomes of the material;

- link up with previous knowledge and interest;

- present the material to be studied, including exercises and activities;

- guide and structure, with guidance and help for learning;

- provide feedback;

- promote transfer - i.e. application to the reader's job;

- help retention, or memory.

It also helps if you provide a variety of material, such as straightforward information, examples, quotations, pictures, diagrams, tables, exercises and suggestions for activity. Your readers will also find the material easier if you present information in three stages, namely

- a summary of what you are going to write;

- the main content;

- a summary of what you have just written.

The style you use is very important. Most experts in this field believe that it is best to be fairly informal, and to address the reader as "you", whilst referring to the writer(s) as "we" (in fact, you will probably have noticed this throughout this book itself, which is a type of package).

Most packages and correspondence courses are produced in written form (hand-outs, booklets, exercises, etc.). However, you can consider other media, including tapes, radio, video and television. These can provide wide access to people all over a territory, and also suit better for individuals who learn more easily from other than written material.

If at all possible, you should consider some means of providing two-way communication as part of a package or course. The usual way is through written assignments, but local coaching and counselling (either individually or in groups) can be very helpful. Ideally, a system of local tutors, coaches, counsellors, call them what you may, could be established. This may well be through involving other institutions in different parts of the territory.

There are other ways of establishing two-way communication, although they have some disadvantages. One method is by telephone - if it is available - such that learners may have a telephone tutorial at appropriate times. There have been experiments in remote parts of Canada with two-way television link-ups, but these demand considerable technological investment, the cost of which might well be more usefully spent on simpler things.

As well as publicly-available materials, an institution might well become involved, on a consultancy basis, in the preparation of materials and resources for use by a specific organisation.

Rooms

An institution can also play a valuable part by having rooms available for managers so that they can come and use them for studying. Ideally a range of rooms can be made available, including reading rooms for individual study, and rooms for working in groups of 5 to 15 people.

Information on self-development materials

More and more institutions are establishing an information base and service, for individual managers and for organisations, on materials that can be used in self-development. You will, of course, include information on materials that your institution holds in its library and

198

can make available (purchased materials and materials developed by yourselves). But you can go beyond that. There are directives and categories of audio-visual and similar packages and you may include some in your library. Furthermore, you can also collect and provide information on materials produced and made available by other institutions, this may be particularly useful in countries where the purchase of materials published abroad takes a long time or can be blocked by foreign-exchange restrictions.

10.5 Suggestions for further reading

Holmberg, B. Distance education: A survey and bibliography. London, Kogan Page, 1977.

Kubr, M.; Vernon, K. Management, administration and productivity: Directory of institutions and information sources. Geneva, International Labour Office, 1981.

Kubr, M. (ed). Managing a management development institution. Geneva, International Labour Office, 1982.

Many bibliographies are available on various aspects of management and training which could be very useful in establishing a basic library. More specifically on self-development, two bibliographies are

Boydell, T.H.; Pedler, M.J. Self-development bibliography. Bradford, MCB, 1979.

And, very much broader in scope

Popenoe, C. Inner development. Harmondsworth, Penguin, 1979 (also published in USA, Canada, Australia and New Zealand). A massive work, containing some 12,000 annotated references.

In this appendix we include details of two ways of obtaining information for your self-assessment. These are

(1)   feedback from other people;

(2)   things that happen ("critical incidents").

1.   Feedback from other people

You are almost certainly receiving frequent feedback from other people - your boss, colleagues, family and friends. Indeed, many of us are more or less constantly bombarded with varying mixtures of praise and criticism.

The trouble is that we do not spend enough time thinking carefully about this stream of feedback. Unless you are very different from most people, you too will realise that you do not really evaluate the feedback that you get. That is, you do not really consider it objectively. It is, of course, very difficult to be objective about something like personal feedback which, by its very nature, is almost bound to cause us feelings - either good ones (for positive feedback) or bad ones (in the case of negative feedback). On top of that, there is the added complication that you will probably also have feelings towards the person giving you feedback, and these feelings - positive or negative - will again influence the way you respond to what that person is telling you.

It is probably true to say that most of the feedback we receive comes to us from our normal, everyday actions.

In other words, we do not actually go out to seek it. On the other hand, it can be useful to be more systematic in the way you seek this information, and there is a simple but helpful way of doing so, which we will now look at.

The first step in the procedure is to list the main people who are important, or significant, to you. You can, if you wish, restrict this to the people in work life, although you will, of course, get a better overall picture if you include others as well, such as family and friends.

You might find it helpful to draw a diagram with the "important people" drawn on it (you locate yourself in the centre of the diagram). This can be a good way of seeing how various of these people relate to each other, by thinking about where to put them in the diagram. How far away you put them from yourself might also say something about which are more important than others.

Whether or not you draw such a diagram, the next step is to think about each of these significant people, and ask yourself "What is he or she telling me? What feedback are they giving me?" It is a good idea to write this down.

You will probably find that for some of them you do not really know what they are saying. In these cases, first of all ask yourself if you are quite sure about that - very often you will find that you really do know, but that you would rather overlook it, pretending to yourself that you do not know.

If you still do not know - then go and find out! This may not be easy; it certainly requires courage to ask somebody for feedback.

You might also find that the people you ask have difficulty in answering you properly. Your request for feedback may well come as a surprise, for which they are unprepared. So it might be a good idea to think carefully about when and how you are going to approach the various people, and how you will put your request.

Also, of course, it will probably be useful to ask the others as well. That is, take those whose feedback you think you do know, and check it out with them. After all, you may be wrong. Perhaps they are telling you something different - or something else as well, that you had not noticed.

Having identified the various messages, you are then in a position to continue to think about them, as described in chapter 2.

2. Feedback from things that happen, from experiences

We can get a lot of feedback about ourselves and the effects of what we do by becoming aware of our experiences, of what is happening.

Again, there is a straightforward method of setting about this.

In the previous section you concentrated on important people; now we can turn to important things that happen - which we will term "critical incidents".

The way to do this is to think of some recent important happenings, critical incidents. In general, these will usually have involved you in a difficult situation, which then either went well or went badly.

If it was a very big incident, it might be as well to concentrate solely on that for now. Alternatively, you might want to examine three or four smaller happenings.

Whichever you decide, the next step is to analyse a critical incident. This can be done in terms of what you were thinking, feeling, willing and actually doing at the time. Write down a description of what happened, rather as if you were telling a story, and note your thoughts, feelings and willings at various points. If you find this difficult, it can be helpful to write on two halves of the paper, or on opposite pages in a notebook, as shown below.

At this point, then, you have an analysis of the incident. Your next step is to look carefully at the information that this presents to you, and thus pick out what it is really saying; what is the message that this incident is saying to you?

Two halves of paper, or sides of a notebook

What happened?	What was I thinking?
What did I do?	How was I feeling?
Who else was involved?	What was my willing - what did I want to do?
What did they do?	What do I think the other people were thinking?
	How do I think the other people were feeling?
	What do I think the other people wanted to do?

Obviously, the message will very much depend on you and your situation - after all, this is self-assessment. You might find that you realise that you need to improve certain skills, or you need more knowledge about something. Or perhaps the incident shows that you become over-aggressive when someone else disagrees with you.

On the other hand, the feedback might be positive - you recognise a strength or ability that you had been unaware of.

The main thing is to use the analysis to tell you something about yourself.

Obviously, the way you look at the incidents will again be influenced by your higher and lower selves. If your lower self takes over, you will be coloured by your feelings about the other people involved, or you might not want to admit certain things to yourself. So try to be open to what is happening whilst actually doing the analysis. Look out for your thoughts, feelings and actions at that very time. Who is in charge - angel or beast?

To convert the analysis to personal issues and questions, you can use a similar approach to the one already described. In this case it involves asking yourself the following questions:

(1) How am I responding to the analysis? How am I feeling? What would I like to do?

(2) Why? In what ways are my angel and beast at work here?

(3) Am I sure? (ask this question several times)

(4) How do I feel about the incident as a whole? Is that feeling influencing my response?

(5) Am I sure? (several times)

(6) So: WHAT IS THIS INCIDENT REALLY TELLING ME?

Questionnaire based on the qualities of an effective manager

This questionnaire is taken from a book that concentrated mainly on the second level of management effectiveness - namely manager as professional, the science of managing.[1] It is therefore a bit more limited in scope than the following one (appendix 3) which is based on the overall outcomes of self-development (see table 1 in chapter 1). However, it does have the attraction of being specifically related to the manager's job. There clearly is a link between the two questionnaires.

The questionnaire is based on research that high-lighted 11 qualities of an effective manager, as follows:

(1) <u>Command of basic facts</u>: Successful managers know what is what and who is who in their organisation.

(2) <u>Relevant professional knowledge</u>: This category includes "technical" knowledge, such as engineering, medicine, agriculture, veterinary science, teaching skills, and so on, depending on your field of specialism.

(3) <u>Continuing sensitivity to events</u>: Managers vary in the degree to which they can sense what is going on around them. The successful manager is more sensitive to events and can tune in to what is happening. This sensitivity helps the manager to behave in an appropriate way in situations as they arise.

(4) <u>Analytical, problem solving and decision/judgement-making skills</u>: The job of the manager is very much concerned with making decisions. Sometimes these can be made by using logical, rational techniques. Other decisions call for the ability to weigh pros and cons in what is basically a very uncertain or ambiguous situation, calling for a high level of judgement or even intuition.

(5) <u>Social skills and abilities</u>: One definition of managing that is often cited is "getting things done through other people". This definition may be inadequate, but it does point to one of the key features of a manger's job - it requires inter-personal skills.

(6) <u>Emotional resilience</u>: The successful manager needs to be sufficiently resilient to cope with consider-able stress and strain that arise from typical managerial situations.

(7) <u>Pro-activity</u>: Effective managers have some signifi-cant purpose or goal to achieve, rather than merely responding to demand.

(8) <u>Creativity</u>: This is the ability to come up with new responses or solutions, and to have the breadth of insight, and degree of openness, to recognise useful new ideas when other people propose them.

(9) <u>Mental agility</u>: This includes the ability to grasp problems quickly, to handle several tasks or problems at once, switching rapidly from one to another.

(10) <u>Balanced learning habits and skills</u>: Successful managers tend to be relatively independent as learners - they decide for themselves what is "correct" and "incorrect". They can also combine abstract and practical thinking, and can also learn from their own experience.

(11) <u>Self-knowledge</u>: Whatever managers do is in some way affected by their own view of their job and role, goals, values, feelings, strengths and weaknesses.

These, then, are some of the qualities of an effective manager. The questionnaire that follows is designed to help you to think about yourself in those terms.

You will see that there is no "scoring system" as such. This particular questionnaire is more open-ended. Instead of seeking a numerical score, you should go through the questions, answering them as fully as possible. Then you decide for yourself what your answers mean - what they are telling you (remember, too, that this is still the first step in the self-assessment process of figure 6, chapter 2). In this way, the questionnaire is designed to help you to explore and examine yourself, rather than to measure yourself.

Incidentally, it can be very helpful to go through the questions with a partner - a friend or colleague, for example. In this way you can take it in turns to ask the questions, and follow up the answers with supplementaries, asking for more information or examples, giving feedback on how you see the other person, and so on.

(1) Command of basic facts:

How much do you know about what is going on in your organisation?

What are your sources of information?

How extensive are your contacts?

How many people do you know in your organisation?

What do you know about the way other people feel about your organisation? "Other people" should include those superior to you, at your own level, more junior to yourself, owners, management, and workforce; customers, consumers, and clients.

Can you think of some recent examples of occasions when you needed to know more basic facts?

How much do you know about your organisation's policies?

How much do you know about your organisation's medium and long-term plans?

What do you do to keep informed about all these things?

(2) Relevant professional knowledge

What do you do to keep up-to-date with new techniques and with the latest thinking in your area?

How much time do you spend reading specialist journals?

How do you get guidance on technical or specialist aspects of your job?

How well-informed are you about possible legislative, governmental, and international changes and the effect these might have on your organisation?

(3) Continuing sensitivity to events

What do you do to make sure that you are tuned in to what is happening in a given situation?

How sensitive are you to the way other people are feeling, or to the way in which they are likely to react? What steps do you take to develop this sensitivity?

How perceptive are you?

How do you make sure that your assumptions about what is going on are correct?

What types of situation do you find hardest to weigh up?

(4) Problem-solving, analytical, and decision/judgement-making skills

What do you find most difficult about making decisions?

How do you feel about having to make judgements in situations in which ideally you would have more information?

What range of decision-making techniques do you have available to help you when appropriate?

Can you think of some recent examples of good and bad decisions you made?

In general, how confident are you in your decision-making abilities?

(5) Social skills and abilities

How much difficulty do you have with other people? What types of such difficulty do you have?

What do you do in situations involving inter-personal conflict?

Can you think of some recent examples of situations in which you needed to use social skills? What happened?

How much do you know about what other people think and feel about you?

How do you respond to anger, hostility, suspicion?

How do you try to ensure that other people understand you when you communicate with them? How do you ensure that you understand others?

(6) Emotional resilience

How do you cope with feelings of stress, tension, anxiety, fatigue?

With whom do you discuss your worries and anxieties?

Think of the most tense, stressful situations that you have been in recently. How did you behave?

What do you do when you become emotional?

How do you behave in situations of great ambiguity (i.e. when you do not know what is going to happen next, when everything seems very uncertain). Can you give some examples?

What do you do to make sure that you neither become thick-skinned nor over-affected by emotions?

(7) <u>Proactivity-inclination to respond purposefully to events</u>

What steps do you take to ensure that you are in control of your own behaviour, rather than allowing yourself to be controlled or manipulated by others or by situational pressures?

In which situations do you tend to be independent and proactive as compared with situations in which you tend to be dependent and reactive?

How good are you at taking the initiative?

To what extent are you thrusting, active, self-starting, rather than sleeping, passive, following?

(8) <u>Creativity</u>

How easy do you find it to come up with new ideas?

How do you feel when all the well tried solutions to a problem have failed?

What do you do to try to see new ways of doing things?

How often do you try out new methods, approaches, and solutions to problems?

What are the most creative things you have done in the past 12 months?

How often do you get seemingly crazy ideas which, on further development, turn out to be good and useful?

(9) <u>Mental agility</u>

How good are you at coping with several problems or tasks at the same time?

212

Can you think of a few examples of situations in which you really needed to think quickly? What happened in each case?

How often do you get sudden flashes of insight, in which "all the pieces seem to come together" to solve a problem? Can you think of some examples of this?

How do you feel when faced with the need for rapid thinking?

What do you do when faced with seemingly contradictory information, data, or ideas?

(10) Balanced learning habits and skills

How good are you at relating theory and practice in management?

Can you think of examples of occasions when you were able to draw general conclusions, or generate mini theories, from your own practical experiences?

Can you think of examples of occasions on which you

(a) preferred to rely on the guidance of an expert rather than trust your own judgement? and

(b) preferred to trust your own judgement rather than rely on the guidance of an expert?

What do you do to ensure that you use a balanced range of learning habits?

(11) Self-knowledge

What do you do to increase your level of self-knowledge?

Can you give examples of instances when knowledge or understanding of how you were feeling or behaving affected what you were doing?

To what extent are you consciously aware of your own goals, values, beliefs, feelings, behaviour?

How often do you stop to consider your own behaviour, its causes and its effects?

213

When you have completed the questionnaire, you can then use the normal method of converting the information to personal questions and issues. This involves considering the following questions:

(1) How am I responding to my answers? How am I feeling? What would I like to do?

(2) Why? In what ways are my angel and beast at work here?

(3) Am I sure? (ask this question several times)

(4) How do I feel about doing questionnaires like this? Is that feeling influencing my response?

(5) Am I sure? (several times)

(6) So: WHAT ARE MY ANSWERS REALLY TELLING ME?

---

[1] Pedler, M.J., Burgoyne, J.G. and Boydell, T.H. A manager's guide to self-development. Maidenhead, McGraw-Hill, 1978. Questionnaire and related material reproduced with kind permission of the publishers.

We now come to another questionnaire, which has been
based on the outcomes of self-development, or qualities of
a developed person, as described in chapter 1, and summarised in table 1.

As has already been discussed, there is an increasing
recognition of the link between development as a person
and development as a manager. Therefore this particular
questionnaire may be seen as reflecting this link - in
effect, it helps to assess yourself in terms of the art of
managing (chapter 1).

The questionnaire consists of a number of open-ended
questions, for which there are no "right" or "wrong"
answers; nor is there a scoring scheme. It is up to you
to decide what your answers mean - what they are saying to
you.

Some of the items have been designed specifically to
help you to decide what your answers are saying to you.
From time to time you are asked to look at your previous
answers and see if there is any pattern, or theme, emerging.

As an example, suppose you have just answered the
question "can you think of some situations when you had
difficulty in getting on with other people? What sort of
situations are these?"

Looking at your answers might reveal a pattern.
Perhaps you will notice that the examples you gave all

involved you in disciplining subordinates - an indication of a particular area of difficulty. Or they might have been to do with your being told to do something you did not want to.

Alternatively, a pattern might emerge involving a particular person, or persons. So it may be one specific colleague you seem to have difficulty with. And so on.

You might also spot patterns in your responses to things that happen - your thoughts, feelings, and actions. Can you see any common thread in, say, when you feel threatened? or excited? Or anything else?

Use all the questions as creatively as possible. Interpret them in any way that you find helpful. Add to them if you want. After all, it is your self-assessment.

There are some other recurring questions. One is to ask if other people would see you as you see yourself - would they agree with your answers (agree about you, that is)? Of course, some might, others might not. If you are rather brave, you could combine these with the "my important people" network that was described in appendix 1, by thinking about what each of them would say. Then check it out - ask them!

The other set of recurring questions asks you to reflect on your answers - what do you think of them? How do you feel about them? What do you want to do about them? This begins to lead you into the next stage of the self-assessment process (figure 6).

Again, you might find it helpful to work through the question with a partner. Whether you do this or work on it alone, do it justice by spending enough time on it. Several hours might be necessary to do it properly. You will probably find it quite tiring, so it might be a good idea to do some of it, have a rest, then do some more.

Since the questionnaire really is very probing, another way to use it would be to concentrate on one limited area at a time. In this way, you could take a specific set of questions and work on those, thinking about what they mean, and so on, through to making some

216

intentions for action, and doing something about them. You could then return to another part of the questionnaire later, and work on that.

Be flexible. Do whatever helps you.

1. HEALTH

(a) Thinking, mental health

(1) What are your basic beliefs about people? Work? Family life? Politics? Your country? Your nationality? Your race? Other nationalities? Other races? Morals? Religion? Life and death?

(2) If you said "I do not have any beliefs about any of these", then think again. In fact you almost certainly do have such beliefs, even if you are unaware of what they are.

(3) Can you see any inconsistencies in your beliefs - that is, do any of them contradict each other? What effect does this have on you?

(4) Where do your beliefs come from? What are they based on? How much are you influenced by others as to what is right and wrong? Do some people influence you more than others?

(5) How do these beliefs influence your thinking? Your feelings? What you want to do? What you actually do?

(6) How do you react when somebody expresses an idea or belief that strongly contradicts or criticises your own? What do you think? How do you feel? What do you want to do? What do you actually do? What happens as a result? (Think of some examples.)

(7) Can you see any pattern in connection with these examples? Do some particular people, or some types of situations, lead to particular reactions?

(8) How do you react to situations of uncertainty and ambiguity? What do you think? How do you feel? What do you want to do? What do you actually do? What happens as a result?

(9) Can you think of some situations in which you have had to behave in a way that went against any of your basic beliefs? What do you think about this? How did you feel? What did you want to do? What did you actually do? What happened as a result?

(10) Looking back over your answers to the questions in this section, do you think that other people would agree or disagree? That is, do they see you in the same way as you see yourself? Would some people agree, and others disagree? Who?

(11) Looking back over your answers to the questions in this section, what do you think of them? How do you feel about them? What do you want to do about them?

(b) <u>Feeling: emotional health</u>

(1) When do you feel happy? Joyful? Excited? Sad? Angry? Frightened? Grief? Threatened? Thankful? Loving? Loved? Hating? Hated? Awestruck? Sickened?

(2) What other feelings do you have, and when?

(3) What happens to your feelings? Where do they go? How do they show themselves? How do you express them?

(4) Can you see any pattern here? Do some feelings, people or situations lead to one type of response, others to different ones?

(5) To what extent are you in charge of your feelings - that is, do you have them, or do they have you? Can you think of examples?

(6) What happens as a result of your feelings, where they go, how you express them, etc.?

(7) How is your inner self? Calm? Tense? Turbulent? Or what?

(8) Does it change? When?

(9) Looking back over your answers to the questions in this section, what do you think of them? How do you feel about them? What do you want to do about them?

(c) Willing or doing: physical health

(1) How much physical exercise do you take? What sort? How often?

(2) How fit are you?

(3) Do you smoke? How much?

(4) Do you drink alcohol? How much?

(5) If you smoke or drink alcohol, what effect are these having on you?

(6) Do you carry out any regular programme of yoga or meditation?

(7) Do you know how many calories of food you actually consume on average in a day?

(8) Do you know how many calories of food you personally need in a day?

(9) Do you know how much carbohydrate, protein, fat, fibre, vitamins and minerals you need in a day?

(10) Do you know how much of each of those you actually consume in a day?

(11) Do you know if you are under- or over-weight?

(12) Looking back over your answers to the questions in this section, do you think that other people would agree or disagree? That is, do they see you in the same way as you see yourself? Would some people agree, others disagree? Who?

219

(13) Looking back over your answers to the questions in this section, what do you think of them? How do you feel about them? What do you want to do about them?

2.   SKILLS

(a)   Thinking: mental skills

   (1)   What goes on in your head when you are thinking? Do you think in terms of words? Pictures? Conversations with yourself?

   (2)   Do you prefer to think things out logically or to arrive at an intuitive solution?

   (3)   Can you think of some examples of occasions when you failed to see the logical consequences of certain actions? What were you thinking? How did you feel? What did you want to do? What did you actually do? What happened as a result?

   (4)   Is there any pattern here? Do certain types of situation lead to this happening?

   (5)   How good is your job knowledge? Are there any areas of technical and professional knowledge you would like to improve? Can you think of examples of situations where this extra knowledge would be helpful?

   (6)   How creative are you? Can you think of examples of occasions when you have come up with new ideas? What did you think? How did you feel? What did you do? What happened as a result?

   (7)   How good is your memory?

   (8)   Can you think of some examples of occasions when you "just seemed to know" the answer to a problem, without thinking it out logically? How did you feel? What did you do?

   (9)   Is there any pattern here? Do certain types of situation lead to this happening?

(10) Looking back at your answers to the questions in this section, do you think that other people would agree or disagree? That is, do they see you in the same way as you see yourself? Would some people agree, others disagree? Who?

(11) Looking back over your answers to the questions in this section, what do you think of them? How do you feel about them? What do you want to do about them?

(b) **Feeling: expressive, artistic and social skills**

(1) Can you think of some situations when you really could not express, show or explain what you were thinking? Or feeling? Or wanting to do? What happened?

(2) Can you think of some situations when you really could express, show or explain what you were thinking? Or feeling? Or wanting to do? Again, what happened?

(3) Is there any pattern here? Are there any characteristic features of the two types of situation?

(4) Do you ever try to express yourself through artistic methods, such as painting, music, pottery, and so on?

(5) Can you think of some situations when you had difficulty in getting on with other people? What sorts of situation are these?

(6) What about situations when you succeeded in getting on well with people? Can you think of some of these? What sorts of situation are they?

(7) In all of these examples, what did you think? How did you feel? What did you want to do? What did you actually do? What happened as a result?

(8) Can you see any patterns here? What characterises those people/situations that you handle well, and those that you handle badly?

221

(9) Looking back at your answers to the questions in this section, do you think that other people would agree or disagree? Do they see you in the same way as you see yourself? Would some people agree, others disagree? Who?

(10) Looking back at your answers to the questions in this section, what do you think of them? How do you feel about them? What do you want to do about them?

(c) Willing of doing: physical skills

(1) How good are you at physical tasks?

(2) Do you ever feel a need to improve your dexterity, to become less clumsy, to improve your co-ordination? Can you think of examples?

(3) For each of these examples, what did you think at the time? How did you feel? What did you want to do? What did you actually do?

(4) Would other people share this view of you? Would some agree, others disagree? Who?

(5) What do you think about your answers to the questions in this section? How do you feel about them? What do you want to do about them?

3. ACTION - GETTING THINGS DONE

(a) Thinking: making decisions

(1) How do you respond when faced with a choice between alternatives, each of which has some desirable points, as well as disadvantages? Can you think of examples?

(2) In each of these examples, what were you thinking? How did you feel? What did you want to do? What did you actually do? What happened as a result?

222

(3)   Do you find it easy or difficult to say "no" to something? Can you think of some examples of times when you could/could not say "no" to something you really knew was the wrong choice? In all these, what were you thinking? How did you feel? What did you want to do? What did you actually do? What happened as a result?

(4)   What have been the two or three most difficult choices you have had to make in the last 12 months? Who and what was involved? What were you thinking? How did you feel? What did you want to do? What did you actually do? What happened as a result?

(5)   Can you see any patterns here? Do you seem to respond in particular ways to certain types of problem or choice?

(6)   Would other people share these views of you? Would some agree, others disagree? Who?

(7)   What do you think of your answers to the questions in this section? How do you feel about them? What do you want to do about them?

(b)   <u>Feeling: keeping going when things get difficult</u>

(1)   Can you think of some recent frustrations, set-backs, disappointments, that you have had? What happened? What were you thinking? How were you feeling? What did you want to do? What did you actually do? What happened as a result?

(2)   What about other forms of unhappiness, suffering? How do you manage these? Can you think of some examples?

(3)   Do you notice any patterns emerging here?

(4)   Would other people see you in the same way? Would they agree that this is how you respond? Would some agree, others disagree? Who?

(5)   What do you think about your answers here? How do you feel about them? What do you want to do about them?

223

(c) <u>Willing: taking initiatives</u>

(1) Can you think of a few times recently when you took an initiative, started something going, stepped in to get action?

(2) Can you think of some times when you did not do these - when you waited for someone else to make the first move? Why was this?

(3) In each of these various examples, (when you did and did not take an initiative), what were you thinking? How were you feeling? What did you want to do? What did you actually do? What happened as a result?

(4) What do you think of this? How do you feel about it? What do you want to do about it?

4. <u>IDENTITY: "It's good to be me"</u>

(a) <u>Thinking: what you know about yourself</u>

(1) Can you write a two or three page description of yourself, including your physical characteristics? Your personality? your strengths and weaknesses? What you think, feel and do in various situations? (You should be able to by now, if you have been answering the other questions properly!).

(2) Why not show this description to some colleagues, friends, family? See how they react to it. You could write it impersonally (saying "he/she, rather than "I", and ask if they recognise the person it is supposed to be describing).

(3) Have you been surprised by any of your answers to other questions in this questionnaire? Why? What do you think about this? How do you feel about it? Is there anything you want to do about it?

(4) Can you think of any situations when you were aware of what you were thinking, feeling and doing, but were unable to use this awareness consciously to affect what happened?

(5) Conversely, can you think of some occasions when you were able to use this awareness consciously?

(6) What about times when, looking back, you realise that you were not aware of what you were thinking, feeling, doing, but when it would have been helpful if you had been aware?

(7) In all those examples, what were you thinking? How were you feeling? What did you want to do? What did you actually do? What happened as a result?

(8) Do you see any patterns or themes emerging here?

(9) Do other people see you as aware or unaware of yourself? Who?

(10) What do you think of these answers? How do you feel about them? What do you want to do about them?

(b) Feeling: How you feel about yourself

(1) In the previous section, you were asked to describe yourself. Now, how do you feel about yourself? How do your physical characteristics, your personality, your strengths and weaknesses, make you feel?

(2) Imagine you have been asked to write a character reference for yourself. What would you say?

(3) In what ways do your feelings about yourself affect you and what you do? Can you think of some examples to illustrate these ways?

(4) Are other people aware of the way you feel about yourself?

(5) Looking over your answers to the questions in this section, what do you think of them? How do you feel about them? What do you want to do about them?

(c) **Willing: who is in charge of yourself**

(1) Do you have any sense of your purpose in life? Where you are going, and why?

(2) If so - what do you think it is? How do you feel about it? What are you doing to achieve it?

(3) If not, how do you feel about this? What would you like to do about it?

(4) Who influences you, what you think, how you feel, what you want to do, what you actually do? Who makes up your "influence network"? (Perhaps you can draw up a chart showing who influences you, and in what way).

(5) Can you see any good and bad effects of these influences? What do you think of them? How do you feel about them? What do you want to do about them?

5. **INTEGRATION**

(1) How much of your time and energy do you put into your job? Your home and family? Your friends? Hobbies? Work in the community?

(2) Are you mainly a thinker? Or a feeler? Or a doer? What sort of balance do you have between these?

(3) Which do you do most - work on your own development or on the development of other people?

(4) Which other people? Are there some who are getting left out of things?

(5) Do you spend more time on getting ready (by developing yourself) or on actually doing things?

(6) Looking over your answers in this section, would other people agree with this view of yourself? Or would some agree, some disagree?

226

(7) Looking at your answers in this section, what do you think of them? How do you feel about them? What do you want to do about them?

So far, then, we have looked at three methods of obtaining feedback - namely, from other people, by looking at critical incidents, and by using special questionnaires.

The fourth method that we will consider uses your whole life as its focus. We often refer to this as "biography work" even though, since it is your own life, perhaps we might call it "autobiography". The purpose of this approach is to try to link your past, present and future in a way that makes sense to you.

As before, we are only interested in the first stage or two of the self-assessment process (figure 6) - getting information. We will look at what to do with the information later in this appendix.

The biography approach involves four steps in obtaining information - namely,

- life events;

- periods or phases;

- themes;

- questions coming your way.

We will now go through these four steps in turn. As with all the methods described in this chapter, you can either do this by yourself, or work with a partner on it.

Life events

First, you need to decide which aspects of your life you want to look at. By this we mean which component, not which part time-wise, since the method involves looking back in time over all your life, or at least as far back as you can remember.

So what do we mean by aspect or component? Well, it may be that you want to concentrate on your work life; that is, looking back in time, concentrating on aspects of your life that are to do with work.

On the other hand, you very well might want to look at all aspects of your life - work, family, friends and so on.

Obviously, it is up to you to decide whether to look at everything, or to concentrate on your work life. However, we would tend to suggest that if you are undecided you might find it helpful to look at the broader picture, by including all aspects of your life.

Once you have made your decision, you should then start to go back over your life, identifying key events that happened. It is often best to do this going backwards - that is, by starting now and remembering events in reverse order.

If you are considering all aspects of your life, then any key events will be relevant. On the other hand, if you are concentrating on your work life, then you should focus only on events that are related in some important way to your work.

There are other aspects of your life you might wish to concentrate on, such as interpersonal events (that is, to do with how you relate to other people), and learning events. However, you will probably find that these provide too narrow a focus to be particularly helpful at this stage. You could also come back and concentrate on these at a later time.

What is an event? Although difficult to define precisely, you should be looking for particular things that happened, that stick in your memory. Events might

230

Figure 27. Life-line

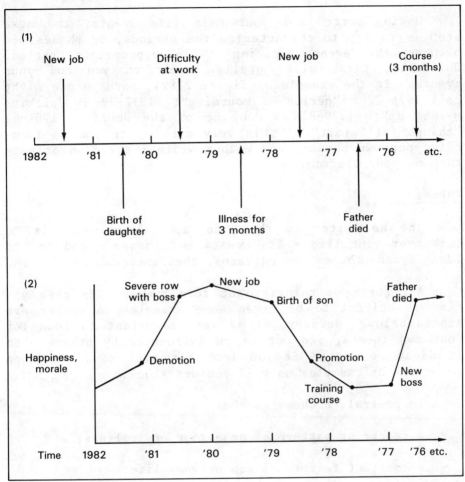

have occupied only a very short time, or they might have lasted quite a long time. Whichever it is, they should be recognisable as definite, separate happenings.

There are various ways of noting down the events. You can, of course, just list them. Alternatively, you might draw a straight line, as a time scale, with events marked at the right (time) points. Figure 27 shows this idea. In this particular example, the work events are on the top of the line, the other events below, although this need not be the case. Another possible way is to draw the line as a graph, with time along the bottom axis, and your happiness or morale, up the vertical axis, as shown in the second part of the figure.

Periods or phases

Having sorted out your main life events, the next step is to try to characterise the periods, or phases, in between the events, giving these appropriate titles. Obviously, these will totally depend on you and your events. In the example of figure 27(2), perhaps one might call 1976-77 a "period of mourning"; 1977-79 as "picking myself up"; 1979-81 as "on top of the world"; 1981-82 "things fall apart". It is very much up to you to identify your own phases, and either write these down or mark them on your diagram.

Themes

The next step in this biographical approach is to look over your life - its events and phases - and try to identify any themes, or patterns, that emerge.

All sorts of things might form themes. In case you find it helpful to be given some examples, a number are listed below. However, it is very important to look for your own themes, and not to be influenced by others. So it might be better if you look for your own, and then refer to the examples only if you are stuck.

In general, a theme can be:

- a recurring pattern of behaviour or feelings;

- a constant feature of you or your life;

- certain tendencies to behave in particular ways;

- particular personality characteristics making themselves apparent.

Here then, are some examples, taken from a number of manager's biographies:

- recurring difficulties with authority;

- a tendency to undervalue myself;

- a pattern of changing jobs whenever things started to get difficult;

- a pattern such that whenever I was faced with a real challenge, I felt I was not good enough to succeed so I gave up without trying;

- recurring difficulties when working with a colleague of the opposite sex;

- always giving way when my ideas disagreed with somebody else's;

- a pattern of avoiding responsibility;

- a pattern of seeking responsibility;

- constantly being impatient for quick results;

- a pattern of seeming to seek out aggressive conflict, as though I am "looking for trouble";

- conflict between my responsibilities as a mother and as a manager;

- often feeling that my strengths and contribution to the organisation are being undervalued;

- frustration because of the difficulties that women managers have in my organisation.

BUT REMEMBER, THESE ARE ONLY EXAMPLES. IT IS YOUR THEMES, FROM YOUR LIFE, THAT MATTER.

You might find patterns amongst the themes themselves. For example

- are there some themes that used to be there in your life, but which now seem to have finished, to have gone away?

- are there some themes that have always been there in your life?

- are there some new themes just emerging?

- are there any themes that emerge, then disappear for a time, then reappear?

Personal issues and questions coming your way

In the biography approach, there are three main sources of questions coming your way. These are

- the general picture of your life so far;

- themes;

- other people.

The third - other people - is of course one of the sources already considered in this appendix, but we will look at it again here, albeit briefly.

First, though, let us consider the general picture of your life so far. Imagine that someone else is telling you about their life, which contains your events and phases. In other words, look at your life objectively, as though it were someone else's.

What would you say to that person, about that life?

- What would you think about it?

- How would you feel about it?

- What would you want that person to do about it - what would you recommend they do?

You will probably find that this is not as easy as it sounds. By its very nature, something as central to us as our own life inevitably arouses strong feelings. It is very hard to remain objective.

Nevertheless, this technique of trying to step back a bit and having a calm, objective look at ourselves is a very useful one. It can certainly help in a number of aspects of your self-development (see various methods in chapters 4 and 7).

So, try to take a detached view - as though you were an observer, or as if you were listening to someone else's biography. This will very probably highlight some questions coming your way from the general picture of your life so far.

Having done this, you can then examine the themes from your biography. These can be a fruitful source of feedback, questions and issues. In particular, ask yourself

- are there some themes in my life that I would like to remove, or at least lessen?

- are there some themes which although "nice", "useful" or "good" at the time, have now outlived their usefulness and should be encouraged to fade away?

- are there some themes in my life that I would like to strengthen, or to have more of?

- are there some absent themes, that are not there although I would like them to be?

Looking at your life themes in this way will very probably raise some questions and issues for you.

Finally, questions can come from other people. We have already examined this earlier in the appendix. If you have already worked through that method, then perhaps you do not really need to do it again - although you may get a fresh view of it having looked at your whole life, particularly as we are suggesting here a different way of approaching this. For example, you might have thought of other people who are important to you - not only people in your present, but people in your past, who are still very much in your consciousness, even if not there physically. These people might well in effect, be saying something to you, or be asking you questions.

As an example of this, one manager on a self-development group could not forget something his previous boss had said. This was still unresolved, and was causing him considerable difficulty. Once he had realised this he was able, in effect to say "Go away, I am no longer at your beck and call", thereby clearing up this "unfinished business". Another common example is if you are carrying, in your consciousness, somebody who has died such as a parent, or child, or friend. Very often there is unfinished business, in the form of some sort of statement to that person's memory, that needs to be carried out. Often this is associated with guilt, which needs to be dissolved. A very useful book in this context is P. Krystal: Cutting the ties that bind (Wellingborough, Turnstone Press, 1982).

In the biography approach, then, questions and statements from other people can be identified by

(1) noting all the people in your consciousness, which therefore includes people who are important to you, even if they are not there physically;

(2) looking at the nature of your relationship with them:

- how did the relationship get like this?

- was it always like this?

- what do you think about the relationship?

- how do you feel about it?

- what would you like to do about it?

(3) asking yourself:

- what are these people saying to me?

- what are they asking me?

possibly checking this out with the people concerned, if you are not sure;

(4) asking yourself:

- is there anything I want to say to them?

- is there anything I want to ask them?

After going though this sequence - events, phases, themes, questions and issues coming your way, you are then ready to move to the next part of the self-assessment process (chapter 2).

At first sight the biography approach to self-assessment is one of those which you would not be likely to do often, or continuously. In a way this is true, but you will very probably find that having done it once, you will gain a lot by coming back to it from time to time. For example, you may well suddenly start remembering different events, or recognising other phases.

Over a period of time you will probably spot new themes, too. These might be quite new ones, or you might see old ones in a new light, changing their character.

Also, of course, other peoples' questions might change - both different questions from the same people, and new questions from new people who, you realise, are now in your consciousness.

Incidentally, you might want to compare your own biography with the developmental issues typically faced during different age-phases, as shown in chapter 9.

Summary of selected methods of data collection
for organisational analysis

1. <u>Observation</u>

   The observer looks at what is happening, watches how things are done, sometimes with the aid of an observational checklist or classification scheme.

<u>Advantages</u>

   - useful for getting an overall picture;

   - may highlight information that will not be revealed by interviews or questionnaires, either because the respondent is unaware, or unwilling to disclose it.

<u>Disadvantages</u>

   - only shows what is on the surface; needs further investigation to explore in depth and to get at underlying issues, problems and causes.

2. <u>Structured interview</u>

   Interviewer plans the interview carefully, preparing all the questions in advance according to a predetermined schedule of what he or she wants to know.

<u>Advantages</u>

   - relatively quick;

   - unskilled interviewers usually feel more confident when supported by a pre-structure;

- lends itself to subsequent numerical or quantitative analysis of data;

- enables data collection to be standardised - i.e. the same questions put to every respondent.

Disadvantages

- closed-ended, and dependent on the framework under-lying the questions;

- inflexible and unresponsive to cues that the respond-ent may give unless these happen to form the subject of a predetermined question;

- unresponsive to other aspects or areas of investiga-tion not considered in design of predetermined ques-tions.

3. Unstructured interview

Interviewer "plays it by ear", encourages the res-pondent to talk, looking for cues and areas of interest to explore with subsequent questions.

Advantages

- flexible; responsive to new areas and data raised by the respondent, thereby opening up the possibility of new discoveries and obtaining a wider picture of what is happening in the organisation.

Disadvantages

- usually takes longer than structured interview;

- requires more skill on part of interviewer;

- less readily lends itself to subsequent numerical or qualitative analysis;

- allows qualitative analysis (although this requires considerable skill).

4. Semi-structured interview

Synthesis of structured and unstructured. Inter-viewer notes down in advance the main areas he or she wants to examine, but allows the respondent to reply freely, playing it by ear to a large extent, following up cues and so on. At the same time, the interviewer makes sure that all the main areas (from the pre-plan) have been covered before the end.

Advantages

- ensures that ground is covered, whilst allowing for flexibility and exploring new avenues;

- allows for both quantitative and qualitative analysis of data.

Disadvantages

- takes longer than structured interview;

- requires considerable skill;

- danger of lapsing either into "must cover all my main points" or of forgetting to cover them.

5. Counselling interview

As with either unstructured or semi-structured interview, but in addition the interviewer reflects back the respondent's answers, and works with the latter on considering the implications. Thus, as well as collecting data, this has potential for actual development.

Advantages

- flexible, may lead to first steps in development.

Disadvantages

- time-consuming;

- difficult; requires skill both by interviewer/ counsellor, and by the respondent.

6. Questionnaires

Investigator plans questions and predetermined data needs, then presents these questions in written form to the respondents. Presentation may be face to face or, more often, at a distance (e.g. through the mail).

Advantages

- once designed and prepared, many respondents may be given questionnaires;

- thus, this can be a relatively very quick way of obtaining data from a large sample;

- lends itself to subsequent analysis:

   . quantitative, if questions are closed-ended, or require yes/no answers, or are of multiple-choice format;

   . qualitative, if questions are open-ended, calling for descriptive written answers from each respondent.

Disadvantages

- good questionnaires are surprisingly difficult to design;

- bad questionnaires are annoyingly easy to design;

- inflexible and unresponsive to answers;

- dependent on framework underlying the questions.

7.   Scales

Instead of questions as such, scales require the respondent to make some form of rating. For example: How often are you consulted about your development needs?

Very often   Sometimes Occasionally   Never

There is a very wide variety of response formats, some of which are included in this book.

242

Advantages

- as with questionnaires, may be used with many respondents, with rapid response;

- readily lend themselves to numerical, quantitative analysis;

- provide a convenient way of plotting scores to feed back to respondents, or to include in reports.

Disadvantages

- dependent on framework or model for designing the items;

- danger of falling into trap of spurious and unjustified statistical analysis;

- surprisingly difficult to design a scale that is in fact valid and reliable;

- extremely easy to design a scale that looks valid and reliable, but in fact is not.

8.   Diaries and critical incidents

In this book, these have been described as ways in which the individual can assess him or herself. As well as this, they can be used at an organisational level, with the investigator collecting in the diaries or records of incidents and carrying out an overall analysis.

Advantages

- require less preparation/design than interviews, questionnaire and scales;

- not dependent on any predetermined structure or model;

- enable real, significant issues to be highlighted.

Disadvantages

- time-consuming and, often, unpopular with respondents;

- difficult to analyse.

9. Role set analysis

Again, this is an organisational level application of a method already described for individual self-assessment (appendix 1). At the organisational level, a whole team group or department works on the exercise together, giving each other feedback about what they expect from each other, and negotiating around those expectations that they feel are not being met.

Advantages

- can be very useful for developing a team or department;

- has developmental as well as diagnostic validity.

Disadvantages

- time-consuming;

- threatening;

- requires skill and commitment.

10. Data feedback meetings

Data collected by any of the various methods is fed back to the respondents at a special meeting. With help of a "neutral" third party (e.g. a trainer), this is then discussed and looked at in terms of members' thinking, feeling and willing.

Advantages

- can lead to movement and development;

- participative.

Disadvantages

- may require many meetings over a period of time;

- usually requires great skill on behalf of trainer (e.g. skills in group decision making, handling conflict).

This questionnaire contains 35 statements. To the right of each statement are the numbers 5, 4, 3, 2, 1, 0. These correspond to the following categories:

5 ...   is a great help to your development
4 ...   is something of a help to your development
3 ...   neither helps nor hinders your development
2 ...   is something of a hindrance to your development
1 ...   is a great hindrance to your development
0 ...   does not apply

So, for each of the statements, please circle one of those numbers 5, 4, 3, 2, 1, 0, according to your view of what it is like in your organisation (using the scoring scheme shown above).

(1) The frankness and honesty with
     which disagreements are dealt with ... 5 4 3 2 1 0

(2) The extent to which roles are
     defined and understood 5 4 3 2 1 0

(3) The overall feeling of friendliness
     in your department 5 4 3 2 1 0

(4) The attitude of your boss when you
     make a mistake 5 4 3 2 1 0

(5) The degree of openness and trust
     between you and your subordinates 5 4 3 2 1 0

(6)   The extent to which you are able
       to express your ideas 5 4 3 2 1 0

(7)   The overall feeling of friendliness
       throughout the whole organisation 5 4 3 2 1 0

(8)   The extent to which you are able
       to express your feelings 5 4 3 2 1 0

(9)   The degree of openness and trust
       between you and your boss 5 4 3 2 1 0

(10) The attitude of your subordinates
       when you make a mistake 5 4 3 2 1 0

(11) The extent to which you are free to
       decide what actions to take 5 4 3 2 1 0

(12) The extent to which you are free to
       challenge existing customs and
       practices 5 4 3 2 1 0

(13) The extent to which your superiors
       respect your views, ideas and
       opinions 5 4 3 2 1 0

(14) The extent to which senior managers
       use their rank and position to make
       decisions 5 4 3 2 1 0

(15) The response of your superiors when
       you admit to a difficulty or problem . 5 4 3 2 1 0

(16) The attitude of other managers of
       the same seniority as yourself
       when you make a mistake 5 4 3 2 1 0

(17) The degree of openness and trust
       between you and other managers
       of the same seniority as yourself 5 4 3 2 1 0

(18) The response of your subordinates
       when you admit to a difficulty or
       problem 5 4 3 2 1 0

(19) The extent to which you feel able
to ask for help 5 4 3 2 1 0

(20) The response of managers of the
same seniority as yourself when
you admit to a difficulty or
problem 5 4 3 2 1 0

(21) The way in which work is allocated
and tasks shared out 5 4 3 2 1 0

(22) The way in which you are praised
or blamed 5 4 3 2 1 0

(23) What happens when you want to try
out new ways of doing things 5 4 3 2 1 0

(24) Your superiors' ability to understand and deal effectively with
people 5 4 3 2 1 0

(25) The quality of feedback you receive
from superiors 5 4 3 2 1 0

(26) The extent to which decisions are
made according to needs of the
task in hand 5 4 3 2 1 0

(27) The extent to which decisions are made
according to the personal wishes of a
small number of powerful people 5 4 3 2 1 0

(28) The extent to which decisions are made
according to laid down rules, procedures,
schedules 5 4 3 2 1 0

(29) The extent to which decisions are made
according to the developmental needs
of as many people as possible 5 4 3 2 1 0

(30) The extent to which you receive
information on your organisation's
performance 5 4 3 2 1 0

(31) The quality of informal meetings
in which you are involved 5 4 3 2 1 0

(32) The quality of formal meetings
you attend 5 4 3 2 1 0

(33) The extent to which you feel that
your superiors understand the part
you play in the organisation 5 4 3 2 1 0

(34) The extent to which your subordinates
understand the part you play in the
organisation 5 4 3 2 1 0

(35) The extent to which managers in other
departments understand the part you
play in the organisation 5 4 3 2 1 0

Scoring the questionnaire

You can either summarise the scores (from various
respondents) to each question (thereby getting an overview
of opinions on specific issues), or get a summary score as
follows:

$$\text{Developmental relationships index} = \frac{\text{No. of respondents who mark 5 or 4}}{\text{No. of respondents who mark 5, 4, 3, 2, or 1}}$$

$$\text{Anti-developmental relationships index} = \frac{\text{No. of respondents who mark 1 or 2}}{\text{No. of respondents who mark 5, 4, 3, 2, or 1}}$$

(These indices will range from 0 to 1.)

In this appendix we will describe some of the things to take into account when running action-learning groups, self-development groups or self-help groups. (With the latter, it will be the managers themselves who run it, without a professional trainer as such.) An outline of these three types of group has already been given in chapter 8. This appendix should be read in conjunction with that outline.

It will be useful to relate the guidelines to the main group phases, namely

(1) forming and recruitment;

(2) trust;

(3) sense of purpose;

(4) commitment;

(5) overall strategy;

(6) implementation of strategy;

(7) closing down;

(8) decision making;

(9) basic processes.

1.   Forming and recruitment

It is most important that members join a group with a good understanding of what it is likely to be about, and what will be expected of them.   Although the final approach to be taken (that is, the strategy to be adopted, see (5) below) will probably be decided by the group itself, none the less an attempt should be made to describe the various options and possibilities that are available.

It is therefore a very good idea to hold a pre-group briefing meeting.   This would be open to anyone who might want to join a group, although at this stage they would not have definitely made up their mind whether or not to do so.   Indeed, one of the main purposes of this meeting would be to help them to decide.

Another point to stress at the meeting is that membership of a group would require commitment - both to their own development, and to others.   This will mean hard work, and quite a high level of sharing information with other members.

You might prefer to hold a series of smaller briefing meetings - or, indeed, talk with potential members individually.   It might also be a good idea to talk with their respective bosses, to explain the idea and get their reaction to it.

It is important to stress that membership of one of these groups should be entirely voluntary.   No one should be forced to attend one, or be sent on one, even if it is thought that this would "do them good"!

2.   Trust

One of the first things that a group needs to do is to start to build a trusting climate amongst its members. This is necessary if participants are going to be willing to talk about themselves, share their concerns, give and receive feedback.

Like all these phases of a group, trust-building is in reality not a separate, distinct stage.   It continues

250

gradually throughout the life of the group. None the less, it is one of the first group issues that need to be tackled.

Much of the trust within the group will gradually unfold, as people do in fact take risks, share concerns, and so on. However, some first steps have to be taken to trigger off this process.

There are all sorts of ways of doing this, four of which are briefly described below.

Glimpses. Each participant is asked to write down, on a piece of paper, ten important things about himself. The participants then take turns to come to the front of the group and write these items on a blackboard, or on flip-chart paper.* They can explain their items if they want to do so.

> *Flip-chart paper is really extremely useful for group work. Used with suitable felt pens, it is cleaner than a blackboard, lots of different coloured pens can be used, and the results can be kept for continuing reference. That is, whereas you have to rub things off the blackboard when it is full, the separate sheets of paper can be kept. Often it is very useful to stick them up on the wall, to remind members what has been said.
>
> Suitable paper is sometimes difficult to find. It should be a reasonable size - 12" x 24" as a minimum. If you have no readily available source of supply, you may have to import it, with all the difficulties that that implies. On the other hand, you might find that your local newspaper will let you have end rolls of blank, unused newsprint, which makes excellent, cheap flip-chart paper.
>
> Sometimes you will find suitable paper - or thin card - from a printing outlet, either a private one or, in the case of government agencies, from the Government Printer. Educational establishments (e.g. teacher training colleges) or ministries sometimes can get it, too.

Another useful type of paper - although rather expensive - is brown wrapping paper: it seems to enhance the colour of the ink.

You will probably have to either import the pens or get them from educational suppliers, although some stationery stores may stock them. For flip-chart work a broad-tipped felt pen is needed.

If you can get it, there is a special substance that is very useful for sticking sheets of paper on walls. When they are taken down, it comes off without damaging the wall, and can be used again.

If you do not have a special flip-chart stand, you can use a blackboard easel. Paper can be clipped to the board, or stuck on.

A variation of the exercise is to ask members to write (on their own pieces of paper) two lists, namely "ten important things about myself that I would find quite easy to tell others about" and "ten important things about myself that I would find difficult to tell others about". They then think about their two lists for a few minutes, and when it comes to writing up in front of the group they can choose any ten from the combined 20 items.

A letter to the group. Participants each write a letter, addressed to the rest of the group. This letter can take various forms. It can be in the first person, introducing oneself (i.e. "my name is -------, I am -------, etc.), almost as though you were giving a reference for another person. In fact, this is probably better than the first person approach, as it gives practice at viewing yourself objectively, which is in itself a useful self-development process.

When the letters have been written each participant can read it out to the group. Alternatively, the trainer can collect them in and read them out, omitting the person's name. Or letters can be shuffled and dealt back at random; each person then reads out the one they now have, omitting the name. Members then have to guess who wrote which letter. (This might be a useful exercise after the group has met for a day or two, so that people have had a chance to get to know something about each other.)

Significant development events. This involves each participant recalling a number of developmental events from their lives, and then analysing them as described in chapter 1 (figure 2). When they have done this, they share their information and discuss it, either in pairs or groups of three. This discussion will require at least an hour.

Further discussion can then take place in the whole group.

At all times it must be stressed that each member is free to share as much or as little as they like of what they have written. There must be no compulsion to reveal more than they want to.

Blind walk. This exercise aims to develop trust by physical means. Members form pairs. One of each pair closes his or her eyes (or is blindfolded), whilst the partner leads him or her by the hand, going for a walk, either indoors or outdoors. The guides have to ensure that the unseeing persons come to no harm. Further, they can make the walk more interesting by getting the "blind" ones to touch various objects (e.g. furniture, plants, trees, soil, cups, liquids, other people.)

After about five minutes, the pairs swap over, so that the previous guide is now "blind".

After the second walk, the group reconvenes and discusses the experience.

3. Sense of purpose

This phase is concerned with trying to sort out more clearly what it is that members hope to gain from the overall experience.

It is important to recognise that individual aims are very likely to change as time goes on. New aims may emerge, or old ones may be seen differently.

So, like all the other phases, although this one might start as "third thing to do", it should also be looked on as a continuous process.

Bearing that in mind, three methods of homing in on purposes and aims are described below.

Self-assessment techniques. Any of the self-assessment techniques from chapter 2 can be used. The questionnaires can be answered individually (perhaps in the time between meetings) and then the answers shared and discussed. Alternatively, the open-ended type questionnaires, based on the qualities of an effective manager, and on the effects of self-development (appendix 3) lend themselves to being answered in pairs, although this would take quite a long time.

A letter to the group. Similar to method (b) in the previous section ("trust"). In this case, the letter should include reasons for the person being there; why he or she thinks that the group will help their self-development, what they hope to achieve, and what they are prepared to contribute.

This last point is important; it is always useful to remind members that they are likely to get more out of the group if they are prepared to put more into it.

Who am I, why am I here? Although this looks quite a simple method, it can be quite confronting and threatening.

The trainer announces that he or she is going to put a series of questions on the blackboard or flip-chart.

You then write up the first question, which is:

"Who am I?"

Members write down their answer on a piece of paper. Then you put up (or read out) the second one:

"Why am I here?"

Again, time for answers. Then question three:

"Who am I?"

This will probably cause quite a surprise! Do not answer any of their questions, or make any comments.

Question four is:

"Why am I here?"

Then:

"Who am I?"

Then:

"Why am I here?"

And so on. Usually about four pairs of questions (i.e. eight in all) is enough. You then discuss the answers, either in the whole group, or in pairs, or small subgroups.

You will normally find that the answers started with names and then general statements about "I am here to develop myself". By the time the fourth or fifth pair of questions has been answered, much more specific purposes are coming out.

Be careful, though. Some people do not like this exercise at all. It is important to help them, rather than punish them.

Paintings and collage. This is another slightly "unusual" way of getting into members' aims. Unlike the others, it does not rely on words and one's powers of verbal self-expression.

Members are given a large sheet of paper and asked to illustrate themselves (a) as they are now and (b) as they would like to be. This illustration can be in the form of a painting (for which you will need paints, of course, and brushes, water, mixing pots; alternatively, you can use crayons) or a collage.

A collage is prepared by cutting out pictures from magazines and newspapers, and then sticking these onto the sheet of paper. For this method, then, you need to provide as many old magazines, newspapers, catalogues, brochures, etc., as possible, as well as scissors and glue.

4.   Commitment

This is not so much a phase as a continuing issue. Members need to be willing both to work on their own issues, and to help others with theirs.

There are not any specific techniques for maintaining commitment. As trainer, you will need to look out for signs of flagging energy, enthusiasm and willingness to do things. Occasionally an ad hoc activity might come in useful, such as those related to risk taking. The main thing is to try to decide why the commitment level is low. Thus, if it is due to insufficient trust, you might have to work on that again.

Commitment to others means being prepared to work on their issues too, even if at times this means doing something you yourself are not very interested in - or even something that you are afraid of. Again, as trainer you will have to help the group with this.

Respecting other people's boundaries is also important. By this we mean recognising where to draw the line, when someone really does not want to pursue an issue any further.

Respecting other points of view is also important. If this seems to be a problem, you might try an exercise such as those related to remaining open.

5.   Overall strategy

As trainer, you can either decide the overall strategy or allow the group members to participate in this decision. The latter is probably preferable, if you can manage it, although it must be recognised that it is a difficult process.

A range of possible strategies has already been described in chapter 8. However, the group itself might well generate some more, and it would be a useful idea to list these on a flip-chart, along with yours, to help make the decision.

Of course, you may well adopt a mixture of strategies. In any case, very often you will find that starting in one particular way inevitably spills over into some of the others. Also, as time progresses you might want to switch to another one.

6. Implementation of strategy

There are various alternative ways of actually carrying out the strategy. In particular, members may

- do things in pairs;

- work in subgroups;

- work as a whole group;

- do various things in the time between meetings and then discuss what heppened when they next get together - again in pairs, subgroups or the whole group.

7. Regular review of progress

It is very important to keep a regular check on the way the group is going, so that you can know you are on the right track or, if not, so that you can take appropriate action.

There are a number of ways of checking out progress. The simplest just involves asking members for their views. Another, similar, way is to get each member to write down good and bad things about the group so far, and then either ask them to read out what they have written, or stick the bits of paper on the wall.

You can also use a simple rating scale. Lots of these are available, but you can devise your own or use the one presented here, which is based mainly on the phases of a self-development group as explained in this book. With this scale, each member puts a mark where he or she thinks the group is now.

When each person has completed the scale, the scales can be stuck on the wall, or scores collected and marked on a flip-chart. This can then lead to discussion.

Here is the scale:

1. Trust

| 5 | 4 | 3 | 2 | 1 | 0 |

High degree   Low degree
of trust   of trust

2a. Sense of purpose: mine

| 5 | 4 | 3 | 2 | 1 | 0 |

High   Low

2.b Sense of purpose: group as a whole

| 5 | 4 | 3 | 2 | 1 | 0 |

High   Low

3. Commitment and respect shown to other group members

| 5 | 4 | 3 | 2 | 1 | 0 |

High   Low

4. Overall strategy

| 5 | 4 | 3 | 2 | 1 | 0 |

Clear   Unclear

| 5 | 4 | 3 | 2 | 1 | 0 |

I like it   I do not like it

| 5 | 4 | 3 | 2 | 1 | 0 |

Working well   Not working well

5. Decision making

| 5 | 4 | 3 | 2 | 1 | 0 |

Effective   Ineffective

| 5 | 4 | 3 | 2 | 1 | 0 |

I feel part of   I do not feel
the process   part of the
                                                 process

6. Level of basic processes and skills

| 5 | 4 | 3 | 2 | 1 | 0 |

High   Low

8. Closing down

A group should not be allowed just to peter out, but should eventually come to a definite end. It may be that when it started a specific number of meetings was agreed on. On the other hand, if an open-ended approach was adopted, you will need to sense out when most people have had enough.

This is actually quite difficult - particularly as you will probably find that some want to continue, others to stop. An agreed, predetermined length is therefore probably preferable. After all, you can always start again with those who do want to continue.

Some sort of review of what people have gained, how they have developed, and what the effects are likely to be for them in the future, is usually called for as part of the closing down meeting. You might also ask each member to write an "obituary" for the group, and read it out.

It is also helpful to ask each person to think carefully if there is any last thing they want to say to any of the other members; this may help to resolve any "unfinished business".

9. Decision making

Deciding "what to do next" always poses a problem in these groups. Although you, as trainer, can take it on yourself to make all the decisions, this will tend to make the other members dependent on you, and will almost certainly lower the effectiveness of the group.

Some sort of consensus approach is to be preferred. This always takes quite a long time, and people often become frustrated and impatient. However, it is worth while in the long run.

To help with this process:

- do not assume that silence means consent;

- check out with every member to see if they agree or disagree, even though this takes quite a long time;

Appendix 8
Questionnaire to identify development needs

This questionnaire includes 31 questions aimed at identifying very common development needs, usually identified across a wide sample of managers. It is related to the outcomes of the various self-development exercises described in this book in chapters 3-8. It can be used in different ways:

- you can use format (a) only and just tick off if you feel a need to work more on a particular aspect;

- you can use format (b) as follows:

  in each case, mark the relevance of this aspect to your job (put "R" on the scale, as follows: 5-highly relevant; 4-relevant; 3-not really relevant; 2-hardly relevant; 1-definitely not at all relevant) and the extent to which you think you have developed this aspect (pub "D" on the scale as follows: 5-I have fully developed this aspect; 4-I have well developed this aspect; 3-I have somewhat developed this aspect; 2-I have not developed much of this aspect; 1-I have hardly developed any of this aspect. If you do not know, or do not understand what the aspect means, leave that item blank.

Aspect of development	(a)	(b)
(1) Command of basic facts about your organisation.		1 2 3 4 5
(2) Relevant professional know-ledge.		1 2 3 4 5
(3) Sensitivity to events - awareness of what is happening.		1 2 3 4 5
(4) Decision making.		1 2 3 4 5
(5) Social skills - working with and supervising others.		1 2 3 4 5
(6) Emotional resilience - ability to cope with stress and tension; inner calm		1 2 3 4 5
(7) Initiative - ability to take action without wait-ing for instructions		1 2 3 4 5
(8) Creativity		1 2 3 4 5
(9) Mental agility, quick think-ing		1 2 3 4 5
(10) Ability to learn, both from others and from your own experiences		1 2 3 4 5
(11) Self-knowledge - your strengths and weaknesses, and how others see you		1 2 3 4 5
(12) Courage, determination, steadfastness		1 2 3 4 5
(13) Sense of security in yourself		1 2 3 4 5
(14) Sense of accepting yourself - in spite of weaknesses and rejoicing in strengths		1 2 3 4 5

262

Aspect of development	(a)	(b)
(15) Ability to remember things		1 2 3 4 5
(16) Ability to think logically		1 2 3 4 5
(17) Ability to handle uncertainty and ambiguity		1 2 3 4 5
(18) Intuition		1 2 3 4 5
(19) Ability to express yourself, to explain your ideas		1 2 3 4 5
(20) Technical skills		1 2 3 4 5
(21) Mechanical/physical skills		1 2 3 4 5
(22) Physical fitness		1 2 3 4 5
(23) Possession of a coherent set of values and ethical beliefs		1 2 3 4 5
(24) Possession of a set of personally significant spiritual beliefs		1 2 3 4 5
(25) Ability to think theoretically, working out abstract principles		1 2 3 4 5
(26) Ability to put ideas into practice		1 2 3 4 5
(27) Ability to listen to others		1 2 3 4 5
(28) Ability to respect others and consider their ideas and feelings		1 2 3 4 5
(29) Ability to go out, take risks		1 2 3 4 5
(30) Ability to think ahead, to plan		1 2 3 4 5
(31) Ability to reflect, to review what has happened		1 2 3 4 5

Appendix 9
Outline of short introductory courses
on self-development

A useful way of helping managers learn about self-development and the opportunities available is to run a series of short courses. In this appendix we are showing an outline for a one-day course and a longer, five-day course.

A one-day course

Approx. time (hrs.)	Topic	Comments and related sections in this book
1 3/4	What is self-development? Outcomes and processes.	Use exercise similar to that in section 1.2 working in pairs. Then discuss, summarising with table 1 for outcomes, and section 1.3 (processes).
3/4	Self-development and managerial competence.	Talk/discussion, based on section 1.2.
1 1/4	Overview of methods of self-appraisal.	Talk/discussion, based on chapter 2. Then experiment with one of methods from the appendices (probably working in pairs.

Approx. time (hrs.)	Topic	Comments and related sections in this book
1 1/2	Strategies and methods for self-development.	Talk/discussion based on section 1.3. Then summary of methods (chapter 3), followed by brief experience with one or two of the methods from chapters 4-8 (there would not be time to complete the method, but it would give a flavour). Allow choice of method, and work in pairs or small groups.
1	Now what?	Summary, and discussion of what it might mean in terms of action for each participant.

A five-day course

1	Introduction.	Various methods - see section on self-development groups.
	What is self-development?	
2	Outcomes: development of self.	Use exercise similar to that in section 1.2 (in pairs).
3/4	Thinking, feeling and willing.	Section 1.2. Talk and discussion.
1 1/2	Self-development and managerial competence.	Section 1.2. Talk and discussion.
	What is self-development.	

Approx. time (hrs.)	Topic	Comments and related sections in this book
1	Processes: development by self.	Section 1.3. Discussion from earlier exercise.
1 1/2	Skills and qualities required.	Section 1.3. Talk and discussion.
3/4	Why is self-development needed.	Discussion based on section 1.4.
	Some methods of self-assessment.	
1 1/2	Give overview, then let participants choose between:	Chapter 2. Talk and discussion.
1 1/2	- people analysis	
1 1/2	- critical incident analysis	From appendices
3	- qualities of effective manager questionnaire.	Work in pairs
6	- developed person questionnaire.	
Depends	Working on self-development Use some of the activities in this book.	Activities, singly or in pairs.
2 1/2	Now what?	Discussion on what to do as a result of this course.